THE SCANDAL OF MONEY

The Scandal of Money

WHY WALL STREET RECOVERS BUT
THE ECONOMY NEVER DOES

NATIONAL BESTSELLING AUTHOR
GEORGE GILDER

REGNERY GATEWAY
Washington, D.C.

Regnery Gateway™ is a trademark of Salem Communications Holding Corporation
Regnery® is a registered trademark and its colophon is a trademark of Salem Communications Holding Corporation

First trade paperback edition published 2022
Cataloging-in-Publication data on file with the Library of Congress

ISBN: 978-1-68451-294-2
Library of Congress Control Number: 2016007726

Published in the United States by
Regnery Gateway, an Imprint of
Regnery Publishing
A Division of Salem Media Group
Washington, D.C.
www.RegneryGateway.com

Manufactured in the United States of America
10 9 8 7 6 5 4 3 2 1

Books are available in quantity for promotional or premium use. For information on discounts and terms, please visit our website: www.Regnery.com.

To Bruce Chapman,
friend and guide for sixty years

Contents

The source and root of all monetary evil [is] the government monopoly on the issue and control of money.

—Friedrich Hayek

Prologue

Winning the Debate

*Humans don't decide what to build by making choices
from some cosmic catalog of options given in advance;
instead, by creating new technologies, we rewrite the plan
of the world.*

—Peter Thiel, *Zero to One* (2014)

Will conservatives win the coming economic debate? The nation depends on it. We deserve to win, after all. We have the best economic ideas, so we say, aligned with constitutional liberty and the American Dream. The economy is in trouble, and after two terms of President Barack Obama the Democrats are mostly to blame.

After a crash like the 2008 financial debacle, the U.S. economy typically takes off on a seven-year boom. "Seven fat years" was the harvest of President Ronald Reagan, who entered office in the face of Cold War setbacks and sky-high interest rates, inflation, "malaise," unemployment, and poverty.[1] Pursuing similar policies in faint rhetorical disguise and correcting Reagan's second-term hike in capital gains tax rates, Bill Clinton delivered a seven-year echo boom of his own.

The Democrats now must answer the question: Why have Americans suffered seven years (and counting) of a famine of growth—the slowest recovery from recession in a hundred years? Why are jobs increasing more slowly than the job force is shrinking, with lower growth in wages and larger gaps in income and wealth than we have seen since the Great Depression? Why are productivity growth numbers at sixty-five-year lows, down to less than a quarter of the postwar average, and business starts actually in decline?

Above all, if the Democrats have governed well, why are our young people demoralized as perhaps no previous American generation has been? Why is the real youth unemployment rate at 25 to 35 percent, even after shrinking the hours for a "full-time job" to thirty? Why do fewer young people than ever look forward to an entrepreneurial future, starting their own businesses and careers?[2]

The crisis we face in 2016 is a fundamental challenge to capitalism and freedom. Will seven years of failure tip America into more of what failed? Or will a vigorous case for a new economics emerge that persuades the average American to renew his faith in freedom? Winning the election requires winning this debate. Why, after seven years of the Obama economy, is the average American worker facing a declining standard of living?

To Democrats, the answers are simple. The global financial crisis arose under a Republican administration and was inherited by President Obama. It plunged the nation into a "Great Recession" marked by an oppressively skewed distribution of wealth, with an estimated $5 trillion in bonuses for bankers over seven years and unemployment soaring above 10 percent in the face of a shrinking percentage of adults in the workforce.[3]

Like most financial crises in history, they argue, this one required active governmental interventions, such as extended unemployment benefits and financial stimuli. But an $800 billion stimulus over three years represented less than 2 percent of the economy. As usual when there are widespread bank runs and financial turmoil, the Federal Reserve had to step in as "lender of last resort," necessarily expanding governmental debts. Needed also was renewed regulation of systemic risks. But our debt levels remained under control compared with those of other countries and in the context of America's world-leading gross domestic product (GDP). Under Obama, a record-breaking stock market and a thriving dollar confirmed other indications of able economic management.

Republicans respond to such claims with baffled incredulity. Yet the Democratic claims are mostly true. To the extent that the economic debate revolves around the usual indices of GDP growth and financial market revival compared with other countries and markets, the Democrats can hold their own. They argue that a more balanced economy fueled by redistributive tax and spending policy can close the growing gap between rich and poor. It can redress simmering middle-class anxieties and lower-class stagnation.

For Republicans to succeed, they first must win the debate. Today they are floundering. Many try to shirk the economic challenge. Intimidated by the media and the academy, they shrink from confronting the most devastating threats to our future. Though Republicans have more accomplished and articulate spokesmen than perhaps ever before, they have fallen into a rut of clichés and forlorn incantations that have not been fresh since the Reagan era. Although they offer inspirational anecdotes, they miss the larger picture.

Republicans have been running on tax-cut proposals since the era of Harding and Coolidge. Tax-rate reductions and simplifications are urgently needed. But again, there is no mention of the key problems of a global economy in decline—of the acceptance by economic elites of inevitable and irremediable stagnation. We have not faced the fact that the Federal Reserve's capacity to command growth is a god that has failed.

GREAT DEBATE

In mid-July 2015, for example, FreedomFest, the annual libertarian gathering in Las Vegas, hosted a long-awaited "great debate" pitting Paul Krugman, paladin of liberal economics and the most popular *New York Times* columnist, against Steve Moore, chief economist at the Heritage Foundation and once the most popular *Wall Street Journal* writer.

The debate had everything. The *New York Times* versus the *Wall Street Journal*, the Ivy League and mainstream media versus Fox News and the Heritage Foundation, academic liberalism versus supply-side think-tank activism, the most prestigious voice of liberal economics versus the tribune of the Koch brothers' libertarianism—all before an avid crowd of several thousand, pumped up by scores of speakers, just off the Vegas strip.

The topic of the debate was "How can we restore the American Dream...for all?"—a question central to the election of 2016. But for many of the attendees, the immediate thrill was to witness the humiliation of Krugman, famous advocate of spending, taxes, debt, and regulations, and Moore promised to be up to the challenge. In nine years and perhaps a dozen debates at Freedom-Fest, on a wide range of economic topics, the flamboyant supply-sider had never lost. A master on stage, pirouetting deftly in argument, juggling numbers with aplomb, dramatically unveiling stark and colorful charts, climaxing with eloquent perorations to the crowd, he was a FreedomFest inspiration. By contrast, Krugman was dour and low-key.

Moore did indeed win the votes of an audience overwhelmingly favorable to his cause. But FreedomFest impresario and economist Mark Skousen boldly conducted a further vote to determine which speaker had changed the most minds. By that measure, Krugman won. If conservatives cannot clearly win economic debates at FreedomFest, how can we win them in the all-important November 2016 plebiscite on the economy?

Moore, seeming perplexed and chastened, discussed the debate at a breakfast meeting the next morning. He had a series of further charts he wanted to show, but he had little to add to his arguments from the day before. Given the enormous ongoing stagnation of the economy, why do conservatives and libertarians currently have so much trouble winning debates with liberals on economics?

The FreedomFest audience seemed startled by the strength of Krugman's arguments. While Moore compared the dismal sluggishness of the current U.S. recovery with the brisk three-year turnaround of the Reagan years, Krugman pointed to larger trends around the world. All countries historically have been slow to recover from severe financial crises, particularly when they cannot lower interest rates, already nearly zero when Obama assumed office.[4] Reagan benefited from Paul Volcker's high interest rates, which broke the inflation trend and provided a powerful lever to promote growth. Obama followed George Bush, who entered office resolved to enact the conservative agenda, lowering tax rates, disciplining government spending outside the military, and appointing many regulators with deregulatory goals. But after a few years of faltering growth marked by a rush of investment into real estate and banking bubbles, the result was a devastating crash in 2007.

Government spending, said Krugman, was not to be feared. In his vivid chart, countries escaped from the recession after 2008 more or less in proportion to their increases in government spending. Second only to dirigiste China, the United States under Obama was one of the best-performing economies in the world. But even China was now in a slump. Comparing economic growth rates under recent American presidents, Krugman showed that the supposed tax-hiker Bill Clinton was the runaway winner, Reagan second, and Obama third, ahead of both Bushes. Krugman conceded that tax policy alone did not explain the comparative data. But perhaps activist government is not the main enemy of the American Dream after all.

According to Krugman, a key test came in the predictions of conservatives and libertarians after the 2008 crash. As he pointed out, nearly all expected the huge increases in government spending and debt to foster runaway inflation and interest-rate spikes that would crash the dollar and bring down the U.S. economy. Many expected the Chinese to bolt from the American currency. These predictions still echoed at FreedomFest 2015 and across the floor of exhibits. Everywhere doom was predicted for the dollar.

As Krugman mildly pointed out, after more than six years of Obama, all these predictions were proving wrong. The dollar was actually surging in value, the stock market was near all-time highs, and interest rates remained near historic lows.

At the post-debate breakfast, the consensus seemed to be that with another half hour, Moore would have conclusively prevailed at last. He had more charts to show and a devastating statement by Krugman in 2003 calling for Federal Reserve Chairman Ben Bernanke to engineer a "real estate bubble" (be careful what you ask for). He would have liked to hear Krugman answer that one. Perhaps all is well with conservative economics after all. Or perhaps something fundamental that is missing can be added.

THE SHARED MYTH OF *HOMO ECONOMICUS*

The most important question that both sides miss is why the Fed's allegedly fearsome economic tools are failing to address the demoralization of Main Street, the debauch of Wall Street, and the doldrums of transformative innovation in Silicon Valley. When capital runs with deep knowledge into effective channels of enterprise, the opportunities of Main Street and the average family multiply. A closed loop of Washington, the Wall Street elite, and Silicon Valley's increasingly political rock stars may enrich the One Percent but does little for America.

Addressing a summit of Republican and libertarian critics of the Fed at Jackson Hole in 2015, Steve Moore calculated that an economic revival comparable to Reagan's "seven fat years" would have increased today's GDP by some $4.5 trillion and raised today's average personal incomes—seven years after the crash of 2008—by some $15,000. With an extra $4.5 trillion a year, Moore asserted, we could satisfy any reasonable needs for safety nets and social niceties.

Many Democratic intellectuals, to be sure, see such growth as an unjust burden on the planet, skewing the climate, bloating the incomes of the "rich," offering a paltry "trickle down" of benefits to the poor, and glutting the nation with unworthy trinkets and addictions.

Behind this clash of cultures, however, demand-side Keynesians and fist-clenched socialists share with conservatives four fundamental beliefs: (1) the economy is chiefly a system of incentives that motivate work, savings, and investment; (2) economic and monetary policy has the power to define the incentives and guide the growth; (3) consumption spending is "70 percent of the economy" and the driving force of economic expansion; and (4) at the center of the system is the human being as a rational respondent to his incentives, a *Homo economicus* reacting to carrots and sticks, responding to stimuli, robotically pursuing pleasure like a psyche in a Skinner Box.

It makes little difference whether you exalt this economic agent as a heroic Randian individual or pity him as a dehumanized cog in the capitalist machine, whether you aggregate him into a Marxian class or agglomerate him into a "grotesque consumer culture." Whether you approach him from the left or the right, you're treating the human being as a passive tool of his environment rather than as an active creator in the image of his creator.

On both sides, the prevailing model of the economy is false. Driving America's jobs and wealth, progress and productivity today are not appetites for consumption or social programs or highway infrastructure or educational subsidies or pavilions of Trump Towers, but a half-century efflorescence of creativity in information technology: computers, microchips, software, communications, and Internet applications. Pervading all segments of the economy, from agriculture to healthcare to government, and dropping in price by at least a third with each doubling of sales, these innovations account for 60 percent of stock market capitalization.

Information technology makes Apple and Google the world's most valuable companies with the largest market capitalization. It is directly responsible for some 17 percent of all jobs and indirectly raises the pay for most of the rest. It shapes such industries as healthcare, energy, retailing, finance, entertainment, and defense. It provides the efficiency to compensate for the mostly rigged or rising prices of an expanding array of government-regulated goods and services, from education and healthcare to banking and bandwidth, housing and social services.

Yet the prevailing economic theory has nothing to say about this creative upsurge in innovation. In the ventriloquist models of politicians, growth evolves from expanding population, incremental investment, material resources, government infrastructure, and education, all spurred by that "grotesque and insatiable culture of consumption"—aggregate demand. Declining prices are not evidence of a learning curve that creates new wealth but a sign of dreaded "deflation." Innovation and creativity are exogenous, coming from outside the economy, mostly from government programs and governmentally dependent universities.

At the heart of these ideas you will find that venerable but imaginary creature *Homo economicus*—"economic man," the rational pleasure-seeker responding to his environment. A better name might be *Homo sumptuarius*, man the hedonic consumer, whose economic choices express his self-interest and appetite for pleasure. Economic theorists caricature as greed any human drive, ambition, and entrepreneurial energy beyond what is necessary for bare subsistence. Since *Homo economicus* or *Homo sumptuarius* could never build that new computer architecture, find that biotech peptide, or design that wireless network, we tell the entrepreneur who did that in fact he "didn't build that."

Surprisingly, *Homo economicus* is not a notion of the Left. Many conservatives sport Adam Smith neckties as emblems of their reverence for the founder of the science of economics. Yet Adam Smith was the source of the idea—inspired by the Industrial Revolution's steam engines, pin factories, and other mechanical apparatus—that the economy is itself a "great machine." Every cog and gear, he said, is precisely adapted to its role and purpose. A cog or gear is even less creative or informative than the rational pleasure-seeking economic man. Keynesian economists translate the great machine into an interaction of massive aggregates of demand, supply, and money.

Most alert to the problem, the Austrian school of economics, led by Friedrich Hayek and Ludwig von Mises, laboriously makes room for human creativity and entrepreneurship, "opportunity scouts" and arbitrageurs.[5] Then they explain it all away as a function of "spontaneous order," apparently restricting human beings to finding price differences and "assembling or reassembling chemical elements" in an effort to restore "equilibrium." We are back again to the great machine purring away as deterministically as the stars and planets of Newton's galaxy.

In recent years, some pioneers of what is called behavioral economics—led by the psychologists Daniel Kahneman and Amos Tversky—have caused a stir by challenging our faith in *Homo economicus.*[6] Kahneman won a Nobel Prize. But astonishingly enough, the behavioralists question the concept only to diminish it further, by denying the rationality that makes the machine operational and its outcomes just.

The putatively rational economic agents—who'da thunk it?—turn out to harbor "biases" and habitual modes of thought, "anchoring" on previous inputs and prices, over-projecting from past experience into the future, overreacting to losses, succumbing to misleading contextual cues. (Did no one know this before?) All these behaviors cause economic players to make bad decisions, undermining their utility for the great machine. The biases, fixations, overreactions, and manias skew markets and perpetuate perilous disequilibria. The great machine sputters, the invisible hand jitters spastically, and recessions, crashes, panics, and depressions ensue. In such markets, justice and growth together fail. Justice, therefore, must be enforced by outside experts, popes, and professors, who much of the time reduce it to a matter of equal distribution determined by envy.

None of these theories has anything very useful to say about technological innovation. To explain the integrated circuit, the laser, the wireless spectrum, the geosynchronous satellite, the Internet software stack, the fiber optic line, the polymerase chain reaction (PCR), the ATM, the carbon nanotube, the defibrillator, or the smartphone teleputer, you must make an imaginative leap into a hierarchical universe, carrying the theory far beyond any deterministic great machine, behavioral skew, or interactive interplay of supply and demand.

Democratic politicians are deeply vulnerable on these issues because they treat innovation chiefly as an issue of justice. They take pains to deny credit to its protagonists: "You didn't build that," snarl Barack Obama and Elizabeth Warren. They and Bill Clinton's labor secretary Robert Reich and most university faculty members insist that today's technological innovation is little more than the fruit of some obscure 1950s research program at the Defense Advanced Research Projects Agency or the National Interstate and Defense Highways Act. Bernie Sanders wants to quadruple tax rates on investment, taking 90 percent of the yields of innovation. Hillary Clinton wants to double the capital gains tax.

Most Democrats see robotics and other advancing computer technologies as job killers rather than job creators, as if more workers would be employed if they were less productive. They see energy production as chiefly a source of pollution, to be suppressed by the Environmental Protection Agency (EPA). They are transforming the Internet into a sterile and litigious public utility regulated by the Federal Communications Commission. They are making the banks into a protectorate of the Federal Reserve Board, which they are turning into a fourth branch of government. All these Democratic extensions of government thwart entrepreneurial job creation. They are the chief threats to the middle-class family's economic well-being.

To prosper, Silicon Valley, Main Street, and Wall Street need to work together. But our misplaced faith in the power of the Federal Reserve to order growth into being by manipulating its monopoly money has led to the capture of Wall Street by Washington and the consequent starvation of Main Street and decay of Silicon Valley. Understanding the real sources of our economic crisis requires surrendering our faith that the Fed has the answers. This is the key not just to political victory but to restoring the American Dream.

Chapter 1

The Dream and the Dollar

A crisis of the American Dream is no minor malaise. It is the dream that brings the American future into our minds and motives today. It is a belief in a world where work and thrift today are rewarded by prosperity and progress tomorrow, where savings promise comfort in retirement, and where our children enjoy glowing prospects on new frontiers of opportunity.

The way monopoly money has savaged these hopes is a great untold story of our time. In an information economy, governed by wealth achieved through learning, money is a messenger from the future—a bearer of information and a signal of opportunity. If the money no longer conveys a reliable message—a way of thinking coherently about our priorities and our values—how can we harbor intelligible dreams?

Today we fear the dream is failing—that something has corrupted the links between our history and our horizons, that some insidious force is stealing our future. But across a cornucopian land, we have trouble defining what has gone wrong. Beyond various volatile indices of GDP and growth, beyond poignant tales of penniless grandparents ultimately triumphant through their proud progeny—*Look at me, on this very podium, a politician!*—beyond a wistful sense of lost mobility, we are left with images of money and its decline.

Money is finally valued in dreams. The past is over and the future is unknowable. Where the dreams go, the dollars follow. Are they all to flow down a new, faintly perfumed, economy-sized American drain? Or can we retrieve the dream of a global monetary order like the one established in 1944 at the Bretton Woods Conference in New Hampshire, which based world currencies on the dollar and the dollar on gold?

Our national morale has long fed on a faith in the frontier—first an expansive landscape, then a Promethean technology. The dream beckons a special people to surmount any challenge and arrive on the shores of a democratic prosperity. "The great cloud-wagons move / Outward still, dreaming of a Pacific."[1]

Because the future can never be fathomed in mere financial terms, we evoke it by summoning poets or novelists or science-fiction prophets for what we call the dream. "Where there is no vision, the people perish." A failure of the dream thus portends an eclipse of the future.

Now giving up on this cornucopian faith, this future, are American academic and political elites. Following a vanguard of scientific activists and economic celebrities, we have arrived at a consensus that the American Dream is a deadly burden for the planet. The very biosphere is said to groan under the weight of American exceptionalism. And the entire globe runs up against what Malthusian fashion-plate pundits call a World Technological Frontier.

All entrepreneurial and technological ventures, according to a canonical paper by the productivity theorist Robert Gordon, face the closing of the world's "productivity frontier." In a dismal account of the limits to growth, Gordon foresees productivity's running into six "headwinds"—demography (slowing of workforce growth), education (diminishing returns of learning as schooling spreads), inequality (with 52 percent of income gains siphoned off to the "One Percent"), globalization (the worldwide reach of U.S. technology pushing down U.S. pay), energy and the environment ("global warming" halting the huge historic growth contributions of fossil fuels), and an overhang of consumer and government debt, perhaps epitomized by the crisis of entitlement liabilities, $120 trillion in the United States alone.[2]

Such luminaries as the former Treasury secretary Lawrence Summers sum up the result as "secular stagnation"—a near-permanent retardation of growth.[3] The Frenchman Thomas Piketty, demonstrating that not all his countrymen share Alexis de Tocqueville's admiration of American exceptionalism, has extended the essential argument into a new Marxian "central law of capitalism." Free markets have reached the end of the line of accumulation and growth, ushering in an era of redistribution and zero-sum reshuffling of wealth.[4]

Spreading this pall of pessimism in American politics is the Democratic Party. In a signature appointment, President Obama named as his chief *science* advisor John Holdren, a population and climate catastrophist who once called for poisoning the water with sterilizers to halt population growth. Importing the Marxian-Malthusian theories of Piketty, Democrats see inequality as stemming from an oppressive and conspiratorial accumulation of wealth. The cause of poverty, the Left tells us, is *wealth*!

Building up faster than wages in accordance with inexorable capitalist logic, the yield of investment exceeds the rate of economic growth. The harvest is an increasingly top-heavy, winner-take-all economy, smothering middle- and lower-class opportunities. President Obama's friend and counselor Ta-Nehisi Coates, from his perch atop the bestseller lists and at the pinnacle of power in America, denounces the American Dream, in terms that echo Obama's previous spiritual guide, Pastor Wright in Chicago, as a "genocidal weight of whiteness."[5]

Evidence grows that in the United States upward mobility and even geographical mobility are being choked off. An American child born in poverty at any time since the 1960s has had only a 30 percent chance of rising to the middle class and only a 5 percent chance of making it to the top 20 percent. That child's prospects would be better even in Europe. Vertical mobility is hurt by the near halt in horizontal movement. The "movers rate" dropped in 2011 to its lowest level since the spread of the automobile after World War I. In 2014 an unprecedented one-third of all Americans between the ages of eighteen and thirty-one had not yet moved out of their parents' home.[6]

Hedge fund philosopher Sean Fieler points out that prime-working-age males have increased their real median income only 6 percent since 1971. With a record low 66 percent holding full-time jobs, the total real median incomes of all men in the their prime working years has dropped 27 percent, while men without education beyond high school have undergone a 47 percent drop.

Mitigating some of these losses are higher female earnings, but exacerbating them are elevated levels of family breakdown.

In response to such developments, leftist economists offer only defeat and despair. They predict a permanent slowing of world per capita economic growth rates. Piketty calculates a 50 percent shrinkage, from 3 percent to 1.5 percent per year already under way, to be followed by a further fall to 0.8 percent. Subtracting incrementally for each of the six "headwinds," Gordon in 2007 forecast an eventual permanent drop of U.S. per capita consumption growth to 0.2 percent. He now points out that by 2012 real per capita growth was already running 8 percent below the level implied by this dismal forecast of 2007.

Many eminent economists cherish the idea that the retirement of baby boomers like themselves dooms the economy. They fret that the declining yield of education, the exhaustion of technology, the rebellion of the biosphere, the rise of inequality, the globalization of markets, and the payback of debt are all grave problems for free economies around the world. Gordon speculates that Swedes and Canadians might remain more buoyant in the face of his sixfold forces of doom. Is it their relative socialism that saves them?

To American academics the data represent a failure of capitalism and a pretext for new interventions. Politicians now move to tap, till, and tamp that "technology frontier." Declaring that the Internet has passed beyond its entrepreneurial phase, a bureaucracy of lawyers and accountants at the Federal Communications Commission is taking it over, putting the net in "neutral," where the government can follow it better, probing all its nodes and prices as a public utility under Title II of the Communications Act of 1934, like an old telephone or railroad monopoly. The

Dodd-Frank Act is an invitation to nationalize the large banks as too big to fail and to marginalize the small ones as too little to succeed. Free of all legislative constraint, the federal Consumer Financial Protection Bureau is regulating all consumer finance, from investment advisors to pawn shops.

Obamacare (also known as the Affordable Care Act) is extending its web of taxation and control over all healthcare, requiring sixteen thousand new Internal Revenue Service agents to make it all work. Redressing the crisis of inequality will be expanded taxation of capital and savings capped by a progressive wealth tax—a program that may begin with Hillary Clinton's proposed hike in the tax on capital gains. Redressing the diminishing returns of education, under the Democrats' trickle-down education theory, is $350 billion more for educators. The waning benefit from globalization suggests "sustainable technologies," more appropriate dreams, and rich reparations for the third world. The headwind from global warming blows on balmy gatherings in tropical hotels where the industrial world confesses its sins and offers further reparations with 97 percent pure unanimity.

Finally comes the debt overhang: well, it can be addressed by more money printing and devaluation and new progressive taxes on any savings and investments that survive the other headwinds.

From Piketty's new Marxism to Gordon's declinism, the dismal science offers convenient excuses for the continuing failures of leftist economics. The warning that these transitory changes in Gordon's anemometer will paralyze progress for the next hundred years is overwrought, but regulatory paralysis occasioned by fear of spurious "headwinds" such as global warming, inequality, and globalization is entirely capable of producing a new dark

age. Even debt is less dangerous than panic-driven high-tax aus-
terity policies to fight it.

According to the declinists, all the numbers began going
south in 1972. Productivity growth sank by 40 percent, from an
average annual gain of 2.33 percent over the previous eighty-one
years to 1.38 percent from 1972 to 1996, sinking in 2014 to 0.5
percent.

From Gordon to Summers, the explanation for the doldrums
is nothing less than a historic watershed in the history of science
and technology as portentous as the eighteenth-century eruption
of the industrial age. Driving the productivity boom for the
eighty-one years ending in 1972 was a unique convergence of
transformative inventions—electricity, the internal combustion
engine, internal plumbing and central heating, fossil fuels and
their transmutations such as plastics, and finally telecom and TV.
Sulfa and antibiotics extended human life; jet engines boosted air
travel. The United States changed from 75 percent rural to 80
percent urban.

According to the theorists, these steps were all singularities—
they could happen only once—and nearly all were completed by
1970. As Gordon puts it, "Diminishing returns set in, and…all
that remained after 1970 were second-round improvements, such
as developing short-haul regional jets, extending the original
interstate highway network with suburban ring roads, and con-
verting residential America from window unit air conditioners
to central air conditioning." Even the computer revolution,
according to Gordon, happened mostly in the 1960s, with computerized bank statements, credit cards, and airline reservations.
Automatic telephone switches and industrial robots also entered
before the 1970s.

The critics of the dream rest their case on a detailed account of the overwhelming and singular transformative power of what they dub "the second industrial revolution" beginning about 1890 (following the first revolution of steam engines, coal, gas lighting, and metals a century earlier). From cars and planes and central heating and indoor plumbing to antibiotics and air conditioners and telegraphs, technological progress doubled life spans, accelerated transport from five miles an hour to five hundred miles an hour, and reduced communications delays from days to seconds. Overall measured productivity rose a hundredfold and growth rates surged.

It makes sense to them that the ensuing productivity slowdown stemmed from a decline of technology from these vertiginous heights. But there is a problem. The only index that identifies 1970 as a technological turning point is the very collapse of productivity growth that the doomsters are trying to explain.

Belying the notion that technological potential declined in the 1970s is the list of new corporations launching breakthrough innovations during that decade. Among the emerging transformative companies were Intel with its memory and microchip revolution, Apple with its personal computers, Applied Materials with its submicron semiconductor capital gear, Genentech with its biotech revelations, and Microsoft with its packaged modular software. The first modern ATMs were spitting out cash. Soon polymerase chain reaction tools would enable mass replication of the DNA codes of life. Ethernet and the Internet Protocols portended a coming transformation of communications.

Also continuing to advance were the technologies of the second industrial age as they combined with information tools. Federal Express launched its overnight deliveries, Walmart its retailing revolution, Southwest Airlines its democratization of the air. Containerization vastly facilitated international shipping and trade. Annual productivity growth, as the advance of GDP over hours of labor, did not plummet from 3 percent to .5 percent because of any putative 1970s exhaustion of intrinsic technological gains.

In an information economy, growth springs not from power but from knowledge. Crucial to the growth of knowledge is learning, conducted across an economy through the falsifiable testing of entrepreneurial ideas in companies that can fail. The economy is a test and measurement system, and it requires reliable learning guided by an accurate meter of monetary value.

The elephant in the room ignored by most of the economists and the productivity experts was the sudden eclipse of money as a meter, as a measuring stick, as a scale of value, and as a signal of opportunity. Through two centuries of fabulous industrial creativity and progress under the gold standard, as even Piketty recounts, every major currency long "seemed as solid as marble…seemed to measure quantities that did not vary with time, thus laying down markers that bestowed an aura of eternity on monetary magnitudes."

How did enterprise move from these changeless marmoreal tracks into an oceanic wavescape of microsecond transactions? How did we change from frontiersmen into "flash boys"?

This predictable carrier of the surprises of creativity, this perdurable channel for productive innovation, gave way like a great dam, unleashing a turbulent sea of fluctuating values. The change occurred on a single, identifiable day—August 15, 1971. This was the day President Richard Nixon permanently detached the U.S. dollar from gold.

As the British politician and historian Kwasi Kwarteng puts
it in *War and Gold* (2014), "Nixon's decision in August
1971…substantially altered the course of monetary history and
inaugurated a period, for the first time in 2,500 years, in which
gold was effectively demonetized…."[7]

The absence of a legal link between the dollar and any physical reality plunged the world into monetary anarchy. With no
dollar anchor for long-term investment, financial horizons shrank
and markets dissolved into trading over bets on bits. Contemplating the 1970s without mentioning this epochal event could be
justified only if it had as little effect as Nixon promised at the
time.

Nixon's announcement was full of reassurances that leaving
the gold standard would "strengthen" or "stabilize" the dollar.
Milton Friedman, who urged Nixon to make the move, predicted
that it would have little effect on the worth of the currency. Paul
Samuelson led a parade of eminent figures forecasting a sharp
decline in the price of gold. That gold in fact quadrupled over the
next three years and rose by a factor of twenty-three before a
correction at the end of the decade illustrated the blindness of
both the economic profession and the politicians in charge to the
metrics and dynamics of money. Most economists endorse John
Maynard Keynes's onetime dismissal of gold as a "barbarous
relic" and cannot bear even to think of its continuing sway in the
minds of men.

Barring any more persuasive explanation, the collapse in
productivity growth after 1972 must be deemed just another of
the cascading effects of the destruction of the information content
of money as a metric. The most salient immediate result was the
abrupt end of two centuries of nearly stable long-term interest

rates in both the United States and Great Britain. With the dollar off gold, interest rates on ten-year bonds began to move up and down wildly, in unprecedented ways. Since time preferences could not be similarly swinging, this instability reflected the new chaos of currencies.

Amid that chaos, the values of assets and liabilities gyrated unpredictably, producing bankruptcies on one side and bonanzas on the other. Because the changes were unexpected and came in the money rather than in the actual performance of companies, the results for most citizens seemed random. Debt burdens surged mysteriously for some and were inflated away for others. Bankruptcies soared. Relishing volatility, the financial sector thrived. Trading triumphed over work and thrift. Inequality broadened, as the top 10 percent of earners jacked up their take from 33 percent of all income in 1971 to 45 percent in 2010. Economic horizons shrank.

John Tamny recounts many of the effects of going off gold in his book *Popular Economics* (2014). One of them was Jimmy Carter's famous "malaise" decade. Oil and commodity prices spiked. The Chicago Mercantile Exchange started a financial futures market for commodities largely to enable hedging by farmers whiplashed by gyrating prices. Hedge funds began their long boom. The yen went from 360 per dollar to 100 per dollar. The U.S. automobile and air transport industries collapsed as the price of oil soared. Manufacturing withered. Governments pushed real estate as a haven from dollar depreciation, turning the U.S. economy from an industrial powerhouse into a financial and consumption casino.

With no global standard of value, currency trading became the world's largest and most useless enterprise, accounting for more than a quadrillion dollars in transactions every year by 2015—a third of the GDP every day. It gobbled up the profits of what is called "seigniorage," the gains from issuing money. These gains represent the difference between the coin's cost of production and its value. The central banks and government Treasuries win most of these gains. But these quantitative changes also lavishly benefit any early borrowers or lenders of the government money who can act before related price changes propagate through the economy. But all the currency trading failed in its one crucial role: it failed to find values even remotely as stable as the economic activity they measured. Meanwhile the public sought shelter and consolation in housing appreciation, which at least was more rarely marked to market. But people suffered a sharp rise in the cost of key human needs—food, fuel, medical care, shelter, and education.

Measuring the extent of the damage were sky-high prices relative to what they would have been under the Bretton Woods standard: translated to a value of thirty-five dollars per ounce of gold, a barrel of oil would sell for less than $2.80, and gasoline might still be around thirty cents a gallon.

Chaos in money stultified the entire economy. To blame technology—the one part of the system that continued to thrive and arguably to accelerate—is simply a way to deny the obvious. The world financial establishment had converged on Richard Nixon and persuaded him to make a tragic and tremendous error.

The middle-income crunch and decline in productivity that still endanger the American Dream began with Nixon's default on gold. Despite President Reagan's and Fed Chairman Paul Volcker's heroic and temporarily successful battle to prop up a viable dollar with supply-side tax cuts and an informal gold price target, "there was no permanent repair of the world monetary system," as Seth Lipsky writes. There was "no restoration of the legal checks on government overreach," no limits to the tempests of short-term trading and trafficking in a surf of meaningless money values. The world economy ever since has suffered from a hypertrophy of finance. Currency trades in the trillions per day and derivatives totaling in the scores of trillions a year divert an ever-growing share of world commerce to bets on the volatility of increasingly vacuous aggregates.

U.S. entrepreneurs fought back, empowered by technology and spurred by tax-rate reductions and deregulation. But during the late 1990s, a wrenching and unexpected 30 percent dollar deflation (a 57 percent gain against gold) temporarily brought down the Internet economy, bankrupting thousands of telecoms that had incurred heavy debts to build out the new networks with fiber optics. Suddenly these debts loomed 30 percent larger from unexpected deflation of the dollar. To this day, most of these entrepreneurs—some, like Bernie Ebbers, still in jail for enigmatic accounting crimes—don't know what hit them. But a long canonical history ordains that unexpected deflation ruins debtors. From Asian builders to U.S. retailers, the bankruptcies tracked debt burdens, and no one incurred debts like Internet telecom in the new age of global fiber optics.

Ever since the millennial crash, the United States has been buffeted by currency shocks, interest-rate gyrations, and financial device bubbles. Government fashions move "investment" from real estate consumption to climate distractions. It was technology alone that saved the world economy. But as Steve Forbes put it, the world underwent "four decades of slow-motion wealth destruction, as the value of the dollar dropped 80 percent."

Dissolved were the maps and metrics across both space and time. The spatial index is the web of exchange rates between currencies that mediate all global trade. This is a horizontal axis, the geographical span of enterprise. Here existing products are replicated across now-globalized *space*—in Peter Thiel's trope, from "one to *n*." The indices of *time* are the interest rates that mediate between past and future—the vertical dimension that takes the economy into the future, what Thiel depicts as the vectors from "zero to one."[8]

Since the early 1970s these once-golden gauges and guideposts have lost their meaning, subject now to constant manipulation by government bodies around the globe and by their increasingly nationalized banking systems. With currencies and interest rates far more volatile than the economic activity that they guide, the horizons of investment and commerce had to shrink proportionally with real economic knowledge. Only China, ironically, fixing on the dollar and focusing its trade on America, managed to insulate a workable monetary path. (In return, it faced constant charges of monetary manipulation.) But the Chinese strategy worked until mid-2015, when even China had partly to give in to the global currency chaos.

Most insidious was the eclipse of time, the flattening of interest rates in a global governmental raid on the future. Government debt seizes assets and moves them to the present. It is justifiable only if the spending on present goods promises a large yield for the future. Debt incurred for near-term stimulus merely depletes the future, bidding up the prices of current assets without improving their yields or creating new assets that can repay the debts. The result is swollen asset values, quantitatively "eased" but qualitatively empty—a bubble. When the prices fall back, the debts remain and weigh down the economy in much the way Piketty describes. But he comically errs in seeing the problem as actual saving and investment rather than government expropriation of the real creators of value.

In the United States, the costs of the policy fell first on the pensions of the middle class. The Fed ultimately imposed near-zero interest rates, giving governments and their cronies free money, shrinking the horizons of future enterprise. This exercise of government power suppressed entrepreneurial knowledge. Corporate pension liabilities soared, and the yield of new savings cratered.

Behind a bond bubble was a decline of returns. With interest rates flattened, government zeroes out the future. Abandoned were 80 percent of private defined-benefit pension plans. Public plans faced a similar evisceration in the future. With no acknowledgment, the U.S. government had casually dispossessed the American middle class of its retirement assets and pushed millions of Americans into acute dependency on government programs such as Social Security, disability, Medicaid, and Medicare. Government dependency negated the American Dream.

Without dreams, the dollar perishes.

Chapter 2

Justice before Growth

If an expensive car crashes into a wall, all the information and value disappears though all its atoms and molecules remain. Value is information. The car is knowledge.

—Cesar Hidalgo, *Why Information Grows* (2015)

Money is the central information utility of the world economy. As a medium of exchange, store of value, and unit of account, money is the critical vessel of information about the conditions of markets around the globe in both time and space. Monetary systems thus can be judged as moral systems—do they lie or tell the truth?

In my last book, *Knowledge and Power: The Information Theory of Capitalism and How It Is Revolutionizing Our World*, I found that wealth is *knowledge* and growth is *learning* and that both are governed by the rigorous science of information.[1] Prehistoric man commanded all the material resources we have today. The difference between our age and his is the expansion of knowledge. Knowledge expands through testable learning, "learning curves," proceeding through entrepreneurial experiments.

Manifesting this process is the learning or experience curve in individual businesses and industries. Perhaps the most thoroughly documented phenomenon in all enterprise, learning curves ordain that the cost of producing any good or service drops by between 20 percent and 30 percent with every doubling of total units sold. The Boston Consulting Group and Bain & Company charted learning curves across the entire capitalist economy, affecting everything from pins to cookies, insurance policies to phone calls, transistors to lines of code, pork bellies to bottles of milk, steel ingots to airplanes.[2]

Growing apace with output and sales is entrepreneurial learning, yielding new knowledge across companies and industries, bringing improvements to every facet of production, every manufacturing process, every detail of design, marketing, and management. Crucially, the curve extends to customers, who learn how to use the product and multiply applications as it drops in price. The proliferation of hundreds of thousands of applications for Apple's iPhones, for example, represented the learning curve of the users as much as the learning curve at Apple.

The most famous such curve is that described by Moore's Law, which predicts a doubling of computer cost-effectiveness every twenty-four months. It has been recycled by the solar industry in the form of Swanson's Law, showing the decline of the cost of silicon photovoltaic cells from seventy-six dollars per watt in 1977 to fifty cents per watt in 2014. The inventor and futurist Ray Kurzweil has put all these curves together in an exhaustive catalog that reaches a climax later in this century as a so-called

"singularity," when the capabilities of computers by many measures will surpass the power of human brains.[3]

All these curves document the essential identity of growth and
learning as a central rule of capitalism. This process has marked
the history of human beings since the Stone Age, yet it is only rarely
addressed by economists, most of whom think prices should go
up. In a famous 1992 paper, William Nordhaus of Yale showed
that economists failed to measure the most dramatically dropping
cost of the previous two centuries—a hundred-thousandfold
decline in the cost of light, gauged in labor hours expended per
lumen-hour.[4] Nordhaus extended the curve from cave fires and
candles to electricity and the power grid. It is now manifested in
light-emitting diodes that extend the power of light into program-
mable display technologies of all kinds.

Growth in wealth stems not from an efflorescence of self-
interest or greed but from the progress of learning, accomplished
by entrepreneurs conducting falsifiable experiments of enterprise,
their outcomes measurable by reliable money.

Rather than diverting profits to politicians, entrepreneurs
who conduct successful experiments keep their winnings. Thus
they can extend their success into the future. Resources gravitate
to those best able to use and expand them. The central law of
capitalism, *pace* Thomas Piketty, is that successful capitalists, not
politicians, control the reinvestment of capital. If the government
controls, guarantees, channels, or directs investment, it is not
capitalism. Pivotal to the investment process is interest rates. For
entrepreneurs to control capital, interest rates must reflect its real
cost rather than merely the cost of printing money. Otherwise the
money printers will dominate investment.

We can sum up the new information theory of money and capitalism in eight principles:

1. *The economy is not chiefly an incentive system, but an information system.* Greed has nothing to do with it, but justice—a system that rewards truth and filters out falsehood—is crucial.

2. *Creativity always comes as a surprise.* If it didn't, socialism would work. Information is defined as surprise.

3. *Information is the opposite of order.* Capitalist economies are not equilibrium systems but lively arenas of entrepreneurial experiment.

4. *Money should be a standard of measure for the outcomes of entrepreneurial experiments.*

5. *Interference between the conduit and the contents of a communications system is called noise.* Noise in the currency makes it impossible to differentiate the signal from the channel.

6. *A volatile market shrinks the time horizons of the economy.* Gyrating currencies and grasping governments are deadly to the commitments of long-term enterprise.

7. *Analogous to entropy, profit or loss represents surprising or unexpected outcomes.* Analogous to average temperature in thermodynamics, the real interest rate represents the average returns.

8. *The velocity or turnover of money is not a constant.* Therefore it's not the central bank that controls the effective money supply but the free decisions of

individuals as they accumulate knowledge and
decide whether to spend or save their output.

In a just system of growth, business must be open to bankruptcy as well as to profit. When government puts its thumb on
the scales of justice, manipulating money through guarantees and
other exercises of power designed to stimulate economic growth
or protect assets, it stultifies this learning process.

In entrepreneurial experiments, the governing constraint is the
scarcity and irreversibility of time. With infinite time, anything is
possible. Finite time imposes the necessity of choice and prioritization. Time is embodied in interest rates (the money value of time),
in budgets (bounded in time), in contracts (with dates and deliver-
ables), and in accounts (time bound). In economics, time is chiefly
represented by money. In the deepest sense, money is time. This is
not merely a play on Ben Franklin's maxim "time is money" but a
truth about the necessary scarcity of money. As an instrument for
keeping accounts, setting priorities, and evaluating opportunities,
money must be a measuring stick rather than a magic wand. It
cannot be expanded or contracted at the will of the sovereign. In
order to explain a willingness to exchange real goods and services
for it, money must be strictly limited in quantity.

Paradoxically, to serve as a store of value, money cannot be
hoardable. A holder of funds can refrain from using or banking
them. But if money is not invested or spent, it eventually becomes
worthless as no goods are produced that it can purchase. Time
is the quintessential Heraclitean stream; it cannot be hoarded.
Time is the basis for Say's Law—supply creates its own demand.
In one way or another, depending on policy, savings are always
invested or wasted.

As an economy grows, with ever more abundance deriving from ever more learning, only one resource grows relatively scarce in proportion. That resource is time. It is the most real and irreversible of all constituents of value.

The expansion of per capita wealth and income in an economy means an increase in choices and possibilities, ways of using your time, claims on your attention. Although some new goods and services increase your efficiency and some extend your years of good health, the growth of an economy inexorably presses in on the residual resource, the hours in your day.

These hours (and minutes and seconds) are what you actually spend or waste, invest or splurge, save or sleep away. Money offers an accurate measure of earnings and expenditures chiefly as it reflects these costs of time. These costs are tallied in two irreversible ledgers—physics and biology: *the speed of light* and *the span of life*. If it does not represent these fundamental scarcities of human life, our economics will diverge from reality and betray us and the cause of justice.

Under capitalism, more and more goods and services are generated and used in less and less time. Governments can pretend that some goods intrinsically cost more (gasoline or gold) or that some should be free (medical care) or that some items are becoming more expensive (education, medical instruments). People with political power can push particular prices up or down (tuition, taxes, or interest rates, housing or high fructose corn syrup or the costs of launching a new business or a new pharmaceutical). But time remains irreversibly scarce and uninflatable. Money with roots in time—unlike our dollars today—forces real costs to go down in proportion to the learning curves across the economy. Declining prices are the natural condition of capitalism.

Even financial inequalities do not affect the underlying scar-cities of time and attention, speed of light and span of life, play-ing out across the real economies of our days. Time is remorselessly egalitarian, distributed with rough equality to rich and poor alike. Registering the radical increase in equality around the globe is a massive flattening of comparative life spans.[5] The rich cannot hoard time or readily seize it from others. It forces col-laboration with others. Without surprises, all time is low value and boring. Entropic surprises are what lend energy and direc-tionality to time and to economies.

Static measures of inequality of wealth and incomes mislead many. Under a rigorous time regime, it takes work to accumulate the knowledge that builds wealth. Learning entails labor. The top quintile of households contains an average of six times as many full-time workers as the bottom quintile.[6] The more "wealth" a person commands, the more time is entailed in managing and investing it. Most wealth is illiquid, defended by barriers of time, property rights, covenants, corporate structures, and payment schedules at the heart of investments and economic growth. To extract wealth prematurely—to "liquidate" it—is a costly and disruptive process that entrepreneurs undertake only rarely. On scales of unequal wealth, comparing the invested funds of entre-preneurs with the wages and salaries of workers is deeply unjust.

When government redistributes this wealth, it upsets the scales of justice that underlie it. Government can properly foster the conditions under which knowledge—yielded by millions of falsifiable experiments in entrepreneurship—grows. But the les-sons too many people learned under communism still constitute the central economic lesson: power cannot command wealth—surprising new knowledge—into being.

Interest rates, for example, register the average expected returns across the economy. With a near-zero-interest-rate policy, the Fed falsely zeroes out the cost of time. This deception retards economic growth. Rather than creating new assets, low-cost money borrowed from tomorrow bids up existing assets today. It brings about no new learning and value, but merely destroys information by distorting the time value of money. Charles Gave of Gavekal explains: "When the bust arrives, assets return to their original values, while debt remains elevated...the stock of capital shrinks...and real growth slows."[7]

In the name of managing money, the Fed is trying to manipulate investors' time—their sense of present and future valuations. But time is not truly manipulable. It is an irreversible force impinging on every financial decision we make. The Fed policy merely confuses both savers and investors and contracts the horizons of investment, which in some influential trading strategies have shrunk to milliseconds.

The lesson of information theory—the new system of the world—is that irreversible money cannot be the measure of itself, defined by the values it gauges. It is part of a logical and moral system, and like all such systems it must be based on values outside itself. It must be rooted in the entropy of irreversible time.

With a theory of wealth as knowledge and growth as learning, the information theory of capitalism holds that justice is essential to growth. Justice is an effect not of the "spontaneous order" that is thought to emerge from free markets but of the constitutional order that is a planned effect of political leadership under the law. Unless citizens believe that the distributions of the market are just, they will not impose on themselves the discipline, devote the hours, or endure the risks and hardships of learning and growth.

Self-interest will lead them as by an invisible hand to collaborate with government in pursuit of special privileges. Greed is the lust for unjust gains. It impels a drive for guaranteed outcomes in an ever-expanding welfare state—socialism not capitalism.

At the same time, without growth, citizens will find their horizons close in on them in a zero-sum world in which they can win only by preying on others. Justice must come first, and Republicans cannot shirk its claims. Justice is not spontaneous; it is what politicians achieve through visionary and prophetic leadership under the law. It is what soldiers and police defend with their lives under a banner of patriotism. It is what mothers and fathers in a fabric of families offer to their children as a path to the future. It is what judges and bureaucrats and teachers ought to provide in their daily administration of the rules of society. The scales of justice cannot be merely subsumed under a banner of growth.

Stifling opportunity and growth for most Americans today is a gross *injustice*. It affects the distribution of wealth, the exercise of power, the management of learning, and the administration of law. This injustice dwarfs all the other items in the ledger of national decline—from shrinking median incomes and deteriorating educational performance to preference for "socialism" among college students and the loss of entrepreneurial ambition among young people.

It is an injustice so vast that its shape is hard to see from within its increasingly suffocating confines. It springs from an implicit campaign among multinational corporations, universities, financial institutions, and government bureaucracies to capture and occupy the commanding heights of the culture and economy while protecting themselves from exposure to its risks.

The agents of this injustice are familiar, from the White House to the Federal Reserve Bank, from the Congress to the corporatocracy, from the Ivy League to Wall Street.

To accomplish these goals, these elites have ceaselessly eroded the concept of money itself. Both government and financial institutions have transformed money from a neutral medium of exchange, a standard of value, a measure of learning and store of wealth into a manipulable lever of power and privilege. The Fed, acting as a fourth branch of government, regulating the banks and financing the government and its affiliates at zero interest rates; the Ivy League universities, embracing a secular religion of climate and "clean energy" that requires expert regulation of all production; the "best and brightest" disdaining manufacturing and swarming into finance, by far the world's largest industry— all these elites have captured scores of trillions of dollars of unearned wealth.

This shift in the distribution of wealth is no tribute to meritocracy: it is flagrantly unjust because it has not, by and large, been earned by any acceptance of entrepreneurial risk or creative contribution. Productivity is the test. Coincident with this shift, productivity growth in the U.S. economy has rapidly converged with interest rates at near zero.

With money as a manipulable instrument of elite control and enrichment, government *guaranteed* finance, real estate, insurance, alternative energy, agriculture, and education. But if investments are guaranteed, they cannot yield learning or growth. They are by definition unjust. On this injustice has been built the economy of secular stagnation. It reflects a great monetary heist and it must be reversed.

But to reverse it, we must first grasp its sources in a deep misunderstanding of the nature of money itself.

Chapter 3

Friedman and the Enigma of Money

The first and most important lesson that history teaches
about what monetary policy can do...is that monetary
policy can prevent money itself from being a major source
of economic disturbance.

—Milton Friedman (1968)

The government solution to a problem is usually
as bad as the problem.

—Milton Friedman (1975)

In early 1988, under the auspices of the Cato Institute, I visited China with the world's leading expert on the theory of money, Milton Friedman. More than a decade earlier, Friedman had won a Nobel Prize for his influential theory of monetarism, which holds that central banks' regulation of the supply of money is a key to growth.

At the time, China's economy seemed to be on the verge of enormous growth, but it was hampered by a simultaneous surge of inflation. Prices were soaring, and poverty was rampant. One year later China's rulers would dispatch tanks against student protesters at Tiananmen Square. The most conspicuous Chinese prosperity was

in offshore islands such as Hong Kong and Taiwan, with lower inflation rates and per capita money supplies that dwarfed China's.
Nearby Japan commanded the largest money supply per capita in
the world and was rich. Was that a clue? Who knew?

Surely Milton Friedman knew. I thought I would ask the
world's greatest monetary economist to explain some of these
enigmas of money. As the billion Chinese emerged from forty
years of Maoist oppression, however, Friedman had other ideas,
chiefly some advice for the Chinese government. He counseled
the communist leaders, as a top priority, "to get control of their
money supply."

No one ever won an argument with Milton Friedman, so I
readily confess that I did not win one then, or later, over the power
of government-controlled money in an economy. As we bounced
in buses through the streets of Shanghai, Milton answered my
every question with peremptory aplomb: "Inflation is always and
everywhere a monetary phenomenon." But what if government
spending and taxes were the fastest-growing prices, as I had written in *Wealth and Poverty*? Friedman insisted: "Control the
money supply and you can control inflation, regardless of government fiscal policy."

I continued to resist the idea that the Chinese economy would
benefit from advice from the world's leading libertarian thinker
to a communist regime full of control freaks to grab control of
anything, especially money. But at that time, I could summon
neither the words to refute Friedman nor the insights to grasp the
enigmas of money.

Nonetheless, China was soon launched on the world's greatest
economic growth spurt. What does this success have to do with
monetary policy? I had learned from the late Stanford professor

Ronald McKinnon that "financial development"—the entrepreneurial creation of banks and other financial infrastructure—is vital to economic development.[1] But aggregate numbers such as the money supply produced by the power of government are far less important. What matters are freedom, property rights, tax rates, and the rule of law, which enable the growth of knowledge and wealth.

Milton Friedman has passed away, but he continues to win arguments in his great books about the free market, from *Capitalism and Freedom* to *Free to Choose*, which still outsell mine by large margins.[2] But with all due respect for the great economist, I would now like to point out that on the issue of money, despite his formidable forensic prowess and his Nobel-burnished credentials, he has been proved wrong.

The new information theory of money explains how and why. It also explains alternative monetary systems that can fulfill Friedman's libertarian dreams far better than his own "monetarism." It will resolve many of the enigmas of justice and growth that currently stultify the political debate.

State control of money has become a force for government economic centralization, wreaking havoc on economies around the globe, whether capitalist or socialist. By controlling money supplies, central banks and their political sponsors determine who gets money and thus who commands political and economic power. Unsurprisingly, these establishments back entrenched economic and political interests against their rivals, contributing to new unchallengeable concentrations of wealth. Reinforced with arachnoid webs of government regulation and control, these combinations of economic and political power are the primary cause of economic stagnation in the world.

Since the economic crisis of 2008, Washington has used monetary policy to effectively nationalize the Wall Street banks and subsidize their borrowing. Enormous sums of investment money are diverted from the real work of learning that builds wealth into currency manipulations and "investments" in government debt. The once-great Wall Street banks in turn subsidize the political campaigns of their Washington benefactors. If Friedman had lived to see what monetarism has begotten, he would disown it. Refuting this rare error of Friedman's is therefore essential to saving the very freedoms that he dauntlessly championed throughout his career.

The economic theory of monetarism is based on the famous equation MV=PT, which is even emblazoned on a Milton Friedman T-shirt that I run in. "MV" is total output—that is, the money supply times its velocity or rate of turnover. "PT" is prices times transactions, or, very roughly, nominal gross domestic product. Money supply is "purchasing media," what you use to buy stuff, liquid funds. The number of times a dollar is spent over a stipulated period represents its velocity.[3]

To simplify a bit, the money supply is usually defined as cash, checking deposits, and money market accounts. Supporting these is the Fed's monetary base, consisting of bank reserves (partially backing up deposits) and all the cash ("Federal Reserve notes") in the economy—often termed "high-powered money." The bank reserves support bank loans, which can multiply the money supply and support economic expansion. The cash can be turned over an arbitrary number of times. Many bank loans, however, have been boomeranging back to Washington to sustain government consumption.

The turnover of money of all definitions sustains GDP, or more accurately GDE (gross domestic expenditures), Mark Skousen's valuable measure of all spending across the economy. Renamed gross output (GO) and adopted by the Federal Bureau of Economic Analysis in December 2013, GDE includes intermediate spending on capital goods and commodities, not just the final sales indexed in GDP.[4] This advance is important to the economic debate because as a share of Skousen's larger metric, consumption diminishes from 70 percent of the economy to around 40 percent.

Friedman and his many disciples persuaded economists across the political spectrum to believe that in the equation MV=PT, the ruling factor is "M." Control the money supply and you command a lever that can move the entire economy in a desired direction. You can maintain nominal or measured GDP (without adjusting for inflation) at any desired rate of growth. Hence Friedman's advice to the Chinese leaders, "Get control of your money supply."

Friedman's monetarist theory explains why the Federal Reserve Board has a mandate from Congress not just to serve as a "lender of last resort" in crises but also to combat inflation and promote full employment. These goals imply that the Fed controls the effective money supply. By manipulating this lever, the theory goes, central bankers both determine the level of prices (inflation) and influence the level of employment and at least nominal growth. That is the creed of monetarism, suggesting that even in a fully free-market economy the central bank is the one institution that must maintain top-down control.

Since every currency has a central bank, the prevailing monetarism enables a different monetary policy in each nation or region. Separating national economies, this system favors currencies floating against one another, with their values reconciled by a global market of currency exchange. Thus, a global currency is "minted" by currency traders in a strange new form of seignior-age. Under the prevailing theory, money becomes a self-referential system ultimately controlled by each sovereign that issues cur-rency. Sovereign moneys compete with one another in markets around the globe.

By assuming that control over the money supply gives the government power to provide jobs and lower prices in each coun-try, monetarism, like Keynesianism, not only invites but virtually requires a government monopoly on money.

But because we don't trust politicians with a weapon as pow-erful as monetary policy, we take that power from the voters and diffuse it among independent panels of experts and trusted third parties, such as the European Central Bank and the Board of Governors of the Federal Reserve System. Thus monetary theory not only denies free enterprise, it also impugns democracy.

For "M" to rule, however, money must have an inelastic ele-ment to multiply or push against. Velocity (or money turnover) must be reasonably stable and unaffected by changes in "M." That is, people must spend their currency at a relatively even and predictable rate, regardless of the supply of money, and banks must loan money chiefly as it is made available by the central bank rather than as it is demanded by entrepreneurs with promising ideas. Otherwise the people (including bankers) could counteract any given monetary policy merely by changing the rate at which they spend or invest the dollars. Why monetary theory disregards this possibility has long been an enigma to me.

Friedman developed a shrewd and plausible answer. He pos-ited that annual velocity is reasonably constant at around 1.7 times per year. He explained this number as a reflection of deep-seated human psychological propensities, summed up in his famous "permanent income hypothesis": "liquidity preferences" (desire for cash) and their inverse, the savings rate, depend on *lifetime* savings and income targets. That is, you save until you hit your target, and then you spend. During your youth you tend to save; in your old age you tend to dissave. Savings is determined not by the availability of investment opportunities or changes in interest rates or tax rates or exciting new consumption goods or inviting savings vehicles but by the immutable psychology of human beings.

The permanent income hypothesis seems plausible on the surface—*No one in here but us sociologists.* But another word for liquidity preference is velocity or turnover. Friedman thus supplied a sociological explanation for velocity that put it outside economic policy. With velocity more or less fixed, the money supply rules. So despite his acute misgivings about government power and his superb critiques of government programs, Friedman ended up encouraging the idea that the federal government's control of money provides a lever for federal experts to regulate and stabilize the economy. (Shrinking from the elitist implications of Fed control, Friedman himself proposed binding the central bank to a predetermined monetary rule, such as annual increases in the money supply of 3 percent, reflecting average economic growth.)

Liberal economists like Paul Krugman eagerly accept the implication of the monetarist creed. Conservative economists pile on. The eminent John Taylor of Stanford wants to tie the Fed to a Taylor Rule, based on announced targets for inflation and unemployment.[5] Even *National Review*'s Ramesh Ponnuru and former Republican Treasury economist David Beckworth have strongly endorsed monetarism in America's flagship journal of conservative opinion.[6] In an article on the crash of 2008, they impugned the Fed for inadequate expansion of the money supply through the "Great Recession" beginning in 2007, when the monetary base of the Fed's so-called high-powered money began an expansion from $800 billion to $4 trillion.

In 1976 Friedman suffered a crippling intellectual trauma that for the rest of his life seriously affected his thinking. The king of Sweden awarded him a Nobel Prize for economic science, specifically for his errors—his monetary theory and his permanent income hypothesis. In an intellectual lapse common among Nobel laureates, Friedman continued to defend these ideas long after their validity had collapsed empirically.

The one thing we know from empirical experience is that velocity is not constant. Not even close. Through most of the twenty-first century, velocity has fallen like a rock one year and soared like a rocket the next. The money multiplier—a velocity enabler measuring how much economic activity the Fed's monetary base or "high-powered money" supports—swings between 3.1 and 12. Over the seven years following the 2007–2008 financial crisis, the U.S. monetary base rose, as just noted, from $800 billion to $4 trillion, but velocity plummeted. In Japan velocity has been sinking for two decades after soaring wildly in the 1980s. In the United States, as Louis Gave of Hong Kong's Gavekal economics asserts, "velocity is eminently volatile and impossible to forecast."[7]

Jacques Rueff is widely known as "one of the best central bankers France ever had" and the author of the immortal line, "Inflation consists of subsidizing expenditures that give no return with money that does not exist."[8] In a speech about Rueff to the French parliament in 1996, the champion of the gold standard

Lewis Lehrman explained, "All of Jacques Rueff's experience as a central banker had taught him...that no central bank, not even the mighty Federal Reserve, can determine the quantity of bank reserves or the quantity of money in circulation.... In a free society, only the money users—consumers and producers in the market—can determine the money they desire to hold [or] vary the currency and bank deposits they wish to keep...."[9]

But if velocity is not constant, then consumers and investors and lenders could counteract any given monetary policy merely by changing the rate at which they spend or invest the dollars. In recent decades, this is what we seem to have done, compensating for and neutralizing every change in the money supply with a nearly equal and opposite change in turnover. Indeed, in an interview in 2003, three years before his death, Friedman finally acknowledged, "The use of quantity of money as a target has not been a success. I am not sure that I would as of today push it as hard as I once did."[10]

Velocity is not an effect of psychological forces outside the economy. It is the active means by which economic agents— people—control money. Velocity is freedom. It expresses the public's appraisal of economic opportunities and opportunity costs. Velocity comes in two forms—pro-growth and anti-growth rises. In anti-growth moves, people flee from financial assets to consumables and collectibles, real estate, and financial shuffles in zero-sum inflationary surges that are not technically measured as velocity but certainly reflect monetary turnover. Positive accelerations of velocity come when investors plunge into actual companies and drive a rapid learning curve of opportunity and progress. In neither case does the central bank control money. We the people control it.

If we control money, then money does not require a sovereign source. Its source can reside outside the political system. It does not need central bank management. Currencies around the world do not have to be separated and allowed to float against one another.

As an almost-forgotten history teaches, it is possible to have centuries of expanding trade under a stable monetary standard, a monetary system that rewards work, savings, and enterprise over politics and pull. With a stable monetary standard, trade almost never balances.

The needed reforms entail treating money not chiefly as power but as information. While government power can increase the *volume* of money, it cannot enhance the *value* of money. And oddly it is the Chinese who most dramatically laid bare the limits of the monetarist creed.

Chapter 4

The Chinese Challenge

Unexpectedly for many, [the emerging world]—with China leading the way—became a robust locomotive for a global economy that was still structurally impaired by the overleveraged advanced economies.

—Mohamed A. El-Erian, *The Only Game in Town* (2016)

China today is a Rorschach test of American leadership. How we respond to its murky mass of conflicting images—great cities of mostly empty skyscrapers next to industrial zones churning with much of the world's manufacturing capacity, military charades and cyberwar aggressions accompanied by monetary statesmanship and wild prodigality, miracles of growth and swamps of pollution, alleged harvesting of body parts from Falun Gong prisoners and a robust Christian population of between 67 and 130 million, capitalist chaos and communist brutality—will likely determine the American future.

Each of these images contains an important element of truth. But leadership entails selection, prioritization, and strategic insight. Trying to respond to all the images at once will produce not a coherent or sophisticated policy but a stream of spastic

39

reflexes, as we have seen in the Obama administration. It blandishes the Chinese for silly and insincere commitments to carbon dioxide abatement one day and the next dispatches warships to the Spratly Islands to discourage land reclamation projects on reefs in the South China Sea. Denunciations of the Chinese for trumped-up charges of currency "manipulation" are followed by obsequious entreaties to participate in expanded Pacific trade or climate change treaties.

Silly tough-guy postures and blind monotheories can be found on the Right as well. Does the incendiary sage David Stockman, President Reagan's budget director, really mean it when he describes the country as "the Great China Ponzi" or as "an entire nation of 1.3 billion…gone mad building, borrowing, speculating, scheming, cheating, lying and stealing"?[1]

And what does Donald Trump have in mind when he bellows, "You have to do something to rein in China. They're making it absolutely impossible for the U.S. to compete"? He cites as a devastating instrument of unfair trade a yuan devaluation of 3 to 4 percent. As the economist John Mauldin points out, "The simple fact is that [before this recent minor devaluation] the Chinese currency *rose* by 20 percent over the last five years." Measured by the vigor of intervention, he says, "the Federal Reserve has been the most egregious currency manipulator in the world" during this same period. "Trump and all those who prattle on about Chinese currency manipulation have the economic comprehension of a parakeet."

Stockman's charge is more interesting because it is based on an array of astonishing figures. It is indeed stunning that China produced ten times more steel over the last twenty years than did the United States and Japan together and "used more cement in the last three years than the U.S. used in the entire twentieth century." His case against Chinese monetary excesses gains plausibility from a reported credit market ramp-up from $1 trillion in 2000 to $25 trillion today. He concludes, "This heedless resort to the printing press" has left China with a "freakish economy" comprising "one great collection of impossibilities that cannot be...propped up much longer.... It is only a matter of time before it ends in a spectacular collapse, leaving the global financial bubble of the last two decades in shambles."

The argument that China's monetary policy now threatens the entire world economy—"it is only a matter of time"—depends on a particular view of the nature and role of money. To what degree do monetary factors determine business and technological realities? That is a question that has perplexed me for decades.

My guide on the subject has long been Robert Mundell. With Arthur Laffer and Milton Friedman, Mundell shaped the Reagan revolution in economics. Believing that reliable monetary values were a necessary complement to low tax rates in enabling economic growth, Mundell was an enthusiast for the monetary stability achieved under the Bretton Woods system. Named after the New Hampshire resort where the agreement was negotiated in 1944, toward the end of World War II, Bretton Woods ushered in twenty-five years of global economic growth of 2.8 percent per year, unequalled before or since.

The golden age of Bretton Woods ended in 1971, when for the first time in more than two centuries most of the world's economies, including the United States, cut all ties to gold. Counseling President Nixon on this historic decision was Milton Friedman, who believed that currencies should float against one another as they do today.

During my trip to China with Friedman in 1988, my own advice for the communists skipped money altogether and focused on freedom. Recalling Mao's duplicitous appeal to Chinese intellectuals "to let a hundred flowers bloom," I told them, "This statement showed [Mao's] incomparable misunderstanding of the powers of the Chinese people." I called for an efflorescence of entrepreneurship: "Let a billion flowers bloom."[2]

When asked what would happen in 1997, when Great Britain was to transfer control of Hong Kong to the People's Republic of China, I said, "1997 is the year that Hong Kong will begin to take over China." At the time, I had no real sense of how this would happen. But the mayor of Shanghai and later PRC president, Jiang Zemin, and Premier Deng Xiaoping led a movement to duplicate the success of Hong Kong in "free zones" all along the coast of China. Beginning with Jiang's Shanghai, these free zones, modeled on Hong Kong, produced what we all know now as the "Chinese miracle."

Conceived by Deng and Jiang, the free-zone strategy contrasts with the largely failed one-zone approach of the Soviet Union. The effort to emancipate the USSR from the center out maximized resistance, provoking bitter last-ditch opposition from all who benefited from the old system. The incentives of the free-zone strategy, by contrast, were just the opposite. Everyone outside the zone wanted to get in. The pressure was on to expand the zones. Jiang also put key military bases in the free zones, thus enlisting sectors of the Chinese People's Liberation Army in the economic liberation movement.

Hardly a Ponzi scheme, this strategy was perhaps the single most successful freedom movement in world history. Yet Jiang Zemin, its leading protagonist along with Deng, was a complex man, presenting his own Rorschach test to historians. Known as an authoritarian, he assumed the presidency after the Tiananmen Square protests and initiated the crackdown on the Falun Gong. An electrical engineer who befriended leading figures in the U.S. semiconductor industry, Jiang spoke several foreign languages and was known to recite the Gettysburg Address by heart. A passionate supporter of economic progress, he correctly saw that inequality was necessary if China was ever to develop.

People who have known Jiang regard him as a great figure in the history of our era, a politician who managed to survive and achieve historic change in the teeth of the treacherous environment of the Chinese communist regime despite his intense admiration for America, its technology and economics. Although Jiang is not Christian himself, his son Jiang Mianheng conditioned his launch of a microchip foundry in Shanghai, called Grace Semiconductor, on the willingness of local authorities to allow a Christian church to be built on the premises.

Back in 1988 I anticipated none of this. But I said that a Chinese revival of freedom would make China the world's largest economy by 2015, the year in which I am now writing. By measures of purchasing power parity (PPP), this prediction has come true.[3]

So what does this success have to do with monetary policy? China's success is a major empirical rebuke to Friedman's monetarism. China never adopted Friedman's monetarism or belief in floating currencies. Instead, it fixed the value of the yuan on the dollar, much to the chagrin of American monetarists, and adopted as its favorite economist Milton Friedman's intellectual foe and fellow Nobel laureate Robert Mundell. A supply-sider and admirer of the gold standard, Mundell believes in fixed currencies. The Chinese named their leading financial university in Beijing the Mundell International University of Entrepreneurship, and thirty universities in China have named him an honorary professor.

As Mundell predicted decades ago, state control of money has become a cornerstone of government economic centralization. Adopted by most of the world, Friedman's float has become an oceanic global market with a trading volume of some $5.3 trillion every twenty-four hours, dwarfing all markets for goods and services.[4] Yet floating currencies have not tamed financial crises or enhanced world trade or eased political conflict. No one can show that they approach real values, since their massive gyrations—the yen-dollar rate, for example, changed for decades at an average rate of around 4 percent *a month*—do not reflect any substantial change in comparative purchasing power or any other measure of competitiveness.

As Mundell writes, "Friedman was wrong when he predicted that under flexible exchange rates countries would not need reserves. Countries need more reserves today...than they ever needed under fixed exchange rates" with Bretton Woods or the gold standard. Mundell predicts that, along with the dollar, the "stock of gold in the world is going to maintain itself as a viable reserve asset for a long time to come." Despite Mundell's critique, government-controlled money is more entrenched than ever, but with the help of China and other emerging economies, Mundell and the believers in fixed or pegged currencies may well prevail in the future.

Money can reside outside the political system, perhaps in digital forms on the Internet, perhaps with a new link to gold. It does not need central bank management. The energy and effort diverted into trading more than $5 trillion every twenty-four hours to "mint" a global paper currency could be directed instead in productive enterprises.

In a world where capital can flow freely because it is expressed in one metric, trade does not have to balance. Capital and trade are complementary factors. When one goes up, the other goes down. Capital is more mobile and flexible than goods and services, and its movements can drive trade movements. A Chinese company has to choose whether to use its dollars to buy a good or whether to invest them in the United States. Today, many Chinese avidly want a stake in America, drawn by its technologies and its constitutional rule of law. Investments across borders thus can shape the trade balance (rather than the other way around, as most economists assume).

Gold is now ascendant not only in China but in many parts of Asia, which has become the new spearhead of world economic growth and capitalism, with tax rates widely running between one-half and one-third of those in the West.[5] China in 2014 was importing a record $70 billion worth of physical gold, passing newly capitalist India as the world's leading gold importer and implicitly relying on gold as monetary ballast for its floundering banks.[6]

To the chagrin of conventional economists in the United States, China has mostly opted out of the floating-currency regime and effectively tied its currency to the dollar. For refusing to float and defending the dollar against Washington's devaluers, China has been rewarded with a huge increase in trade with the United States. It is for muting currency changes and supporting the dollar that China incurs continual charges of "currency manipulation" from American politicians and government officials who advocate constant currency manipulation by the Federal Reserve.

Nonetheless, while attempting to appease a long list of utterly unappeasable foes—Iran, North Korea, Hamas, Hezbollah, Cuba, and even the fractious followers of Hugo Chávez—the United States all too often treats China, perhaps our most important economic partner, as an adversary because it defies us on global warming, dollar devaluation, and Internet policy.

The browbeating began in June 2010 in Beijing when Treasury Secretary Timothy Geithner drilled in on Premier Wen Jiabao, who recoiled like a man cornered by a crank at a cocktail party. Mr. Geithner's harangue was focused on two highly questionable concerns, neither arguably in the interests of either country: the need to suppress energy output for the sake of the global climate—a subject on which Mr. Geithner has no expertise—and the need for a Chinese dollar devaluation against the yuan, of which one can scarcely imagine that he can persuade Chinese holders of several trillion dollars of reserves. Five years later, China finally did allow market forces to influence its currency. The result was its depreciation against the dollar, utterly contrary to American complaints during that time.

Our case against China with respect to the Internet is also overwrought. Although commanding twice as many Internet users as we do and, with Taiwan, producing comparable amounts of Internet gear, China originates fewer viruses and scams than does the United States. An authoritarian regime, China obviously will not be amenable to an open and anonymous Internet. Protecting information on the Internet is a responsibility of U.S. corporations and their security tools, not the State Department.

Yes, the Chinese at times seem needlessly aggressive in deploying missiles aimed at Taiwan and in their claims of territorial waters in the Pacific. But there is no prospect of successful U.S. military action in that region, and sending Taiwan new weapons is a needless provocation that does not contribute to the defense of the United States or Taiwan.

A serious foreign policy would recognize that the current Chinese regime is the best we can expect from that country. The Chinese revitalization of Asian capitalism remains the most important positive event in the world in the last thirty years, releasing a billion people from penury and oppression and transforming China from a communist enemy of the United States into an indispensable capitalist partner. It is ironic that liberals who once welcomed appeasement of the monstrous regime of Mao Zedong now become openly bellicose over murky incidents of Internet hacking.

With millions of Islamists on its borders and within them, China is nearly as threatened by radical Islam as we are. It has a huge stake in the global capitalist economy that Islamic terrorists aim to overthrow, and China is so heavily dependent on Taiwanese manufacturing and so intertwined with Taiwan's industry that its military threat to the island is mostly theater. Although some Taiwanese politicians still dream of permanent independence, the island's world-beating entrepreneurs have long since laid their bets on links to the mainland. Two-thirds of Taiwanese companies—some ten thousand—have made significant investments in China over the last decade, totaling $400 billion. Three-quarters of a million Taiwanese reside in China for more than 180 days a year.

Including Taiwan, greater China is the world's leading manufacturer and assembler of microchips, computers, and the network equipment on which the Internet subsists. Virtually all U.S. advanced electronics, as the eminent chemist Arthur Robinson has reported in his newsletter *Access to Energy*, are dependent on rare earth elements to enhance the performance of microchips, elements that are held in a near-global monopoly by the Chinese firm Baotou Steel Rare-Earth Hi-Tech Company in Mongolia.

The United States is as dependent on China for its economic and military health as China is dependent on the United States for its key markets, reserve finance, and global capitalist trading regime. It would be self-destructive folly to sacrifice the synergy at the heart of global capitalism in order to gain concessions on global warming, dollar weakening, or Internet politics. How many enemies do we need?

To David Stockman, none of this matters much, because China is a paper tiger: "The 25 year growth boom in China is just a giant, credit driven Ponzi." As he sums it up, "Any fool can run a central bank printing press until it glows white hot."[7]

Stockman's idea of "any fool" is Zhou Xiaochuan, since 2002 the chairman of the People's Bank of China and manager of their monetary policy. Stockman imagines that Wall Street sees Zhou "as an Asian version of Janet Yellen who wears trousers and dyes his hair black." Although Stockman is an inspired critic of Wall Street and the Fed, he seems to have no inkling of the achievements of Zhou and his team.

With advanced degrees in both chemistry and computer science, Zhou was a key part of Jiang Zemin's free-zone strategy in Shanghai that was the heart of the Chinese miracle. In recent decades, Zhou has become a sophisticated monetary theorist and trenchant critic of the floating-currency regime supported in the West. The author of scores of papers and monographs on monetary policy, he delivered a visionary address on March 24, 2009, calling for an end to freely floating currencies and a revival of Keynes's "bancor" proposal made at Bretton Woods in 1944. Tied to gold, bancor would serve as a single measuring stick used to value all transactions in international commerce and gauge all international flows of goods and capital.

Largely under Zhou's economic leadership, China's private sector outstripped its stagnant state-run enterprises to such an extent that government spending has now dropped to under 17 percent of GDP, compared with 26 percent in the United States. The Chinese have even privatized their post office. Meanwhile, the United States has been expanding state controls over public companies under the costly and destructive Sarbanes-Oxley accounting rules, fair disclosure speech controls, and other self-defeating regulations, gravely impairing its initial public offering (IPO) market. IPOs have long served as the heart of America's entrepreneurial economy and the NASDAQ exchange. Jiang Zemin called it "the crown jewel of all that is great about America." Under Jiang's disciple Zhou, China has been emancipating its stock exchanges and connecting its new NASDAQ counterpart in free-zone Shenzhen to the long-thriving Hong Kong exchange. In 2015 China easily surpassed the United States in IPOs. In the first half of 2015, China had 221 IPOs, worth $39 billion. There were fewer than half that number in the United States, ninety-six, valued at $19.68 billion. In quality, moreover, the Chinese IPOs were more formidable in many ways than the American froth of Internet and gaming stocks.

The Chinese lead in IPOs portends an eventual challenge in venture capital. China has recently passed Europe in deal count and tripled Europe in venture funds raised. China lags the U.S. venture industry by about 45 percent in money and deal count, but much of Silicon Valley's investment has gone to some eighty "unicorns," with valuations over a billion dollars, which have shunned the overregulated U.S. public market. This is a bizarre and unsustainable situation. Venture capital cannot function without liquidity events. Unless the United States follows China and begins to deregulate its public companies, China will soon take the lead in venture capital as well.

The innovative venture capital culture of Silicon Valley, capped by IPOs, has long been the prime source of growth in the U.S. economy, providing 21 percent of GDP, 17 percent of jobs, and perhaps 60 percent of stock market capitalization. The current regulatory regime, from the Securities and Exchange Commission (SEC) to the Food and Drug Administration to the Environmental Protection Agency, is stifling this engine of American growth and power. With China now reporting lower government spending than the United States, along with potential leadership in venture capital and IPOs, Americans are foolhardy to imagine that China will long remain behind.

China remains a complex challenge because it is a combination of wildly disparate elements. In evolutionary terms, below a mostly modern technocratic capitalism it harbors a kind of vestigial reptilian brain, represented by its ruling military and party apparatchiks. Among them are the "bunch of communist party hacks" that in Stockman's caricature "have an iron grip on state power...but [no] grasp of the fundamentals of economic law and sound finance." They do control vast regions of the country, but they do not dominate the rapidly emerging Chinese culture of enterprise, which for all its flaws and excesses is rapidly moving toward ascendancy in the world economy.

China's economic achievement, which has moved more people out of poverty than any country has ever done, proves that Jiang was right. Economic progress can definitely precede political democratization. Since 1982, when Deng Xiaoping declared that "to get rich is glorious," China's city dwellers have increased their incomes fourteenfold.[8] Now the challenge is to show that a communist regime can use capitalist freedoms to expand democracy and civil liberty, which should be the next step for Jiang's free-zone strategy. But our next step should be to address China's critique of our own manipulative monetary policy.

A key reason why China has led the world in growth for twenty-five years has been its rejection of American monetary advice. Following Mundell's inspiration, it has mostly forgone the monetary twists and tricks concocted by other Western economists and instead fixed its currency on the dollar.

As Zhou would readily acknowledge, this is not the optimal solution. But with both Reagan and Clinton following a "strong dollar policy," this Chinese fix made U.S.-China trade the pivot of world economic growth and progress. Following Mundell's guidance, China has trumped America's long embrace of an obsolete monetarism. China has reined in its central bank, but America has paid dearly for clinging to the monetarist delusion.

Chapter 5

The High Cost of
Bad Money

*The government monopoly of money leads not just to
the suppression of innovation and experiment, not just to
inflation and debasement, not just to financial crises, but
to inequality too.*

—Matt Ridley, *The Evolution of Everything* (2015)

This decade of the financial crisis—the "Great Recession," with constant rumors and alarms of war—saw an epochal confrontation between the dollar and gold. At first, through 2011, gold surged and the dollar merely survived. Goldbugs claimed vindication.

In a series of ardent books and speeches, the brilliant libertarian polemicist Peter Schiff predicted the total destruction of the dollar and the massive appreciation of precious metals.[1] The Internet seethed with predictions of the collapse of all fiat, or paper, currencies.

Many of the warnings were intended to sell various gold-based products. But the doomsayers were honest in their belief that the dollar could not survive the Fed's fivefold increase in its dollar holdings of "high-powered" reserves. Many imagined that

China and other holders and users of massive dollar reserves would join to overthrow the American dollar's hegemony as the world's reserve currency.

And then, against all odds, at least as understood by hard-money economists and bullion enthusiasts, what eventually cracked and crashed was not the dollar but gold. From 2012 to 2014, the precious metal lost 40 percent of its value against the dollar, which went on an awesome tear against nearly all the world's currencies and commodities. Today it handles more than 60 percent of world trade, denominates more than half the market capitalization of world stocks, and partakes in 87 percent of global currency trades.[2]

To advocates of paper, the lesson seemed unanswerable. Even in a global monetary crisis, exacerbated by wildly loose monetary policy in Washington, with quantitative easing following stimulative buying, and with an explicit zero-interest-rate policy, the full faith and credit of the U.S. government behind the dollar roundly trumped the intrinsic value and scarcity of gold.

Paul Krugman gloated mercilessly in his *New York Times* column. He seemed to have a point. He rubbed in his argument by regularly quoting Milton Friedman's case for floating currencies.[3] Friedman held that floating currencies could respond to real changes in the economy far faster and more easily than real factors could adjust to a fixed standard. With an acute imbalance of trade, it was radically more efficient to change simply one outside price—the exchange rate of the currency—than to change every internal price, every wage, every pension and salary, the cost of every item in the grocery store, and every rent payment—one at a time—across an entire economy.

Radical surgery becomes imperative when a nation adopts economic policies that disable its businesses in international competition. Rather than merely devaluing the currency so the nation could import fewer foreign goods and export more goods overseas (thus rebalancing its trade), a nation under a gold standard would have to change its most self-defeating policies. Otherwise the miscreant country would have to force down all at once its wages, salaries, costs, prices, and government spending—nearly impossible in democratic politics.

Krugman clinched his argument by comparing the experience of the United States with that of Europe during the Great Recession. Europe attempted to enforce the rule of a single currency, the euro, on seventeen nation-states. No floating permitted. This campaign seemed to mimic on a continental scale the effect of a gold standard globally. Krugman pointed out that American states vary as drastically in their economic performance as European states do—Texas and North Dakota booming with energy gains while Florida and Nevada crash with the popping of their real estate bubbles—but the states that suffered the most from the crash benefited from federal cushions supplied by more prosperous states.[4]

Federal welfare, medical, education, Social Security, unemployment, disability, and disaster relief benefits, as well as dozens of other subventions, compensated for recessionary tax revenue losses and cutbacks in state programs. The $800 billion Troubled Asset Relief Program bailed out state governments. Meanwhile, in the eurozone, countries such as Greece, Ireland, Spain, and Portugal faced acute shrinkage of their social services and welfare systems in exchange for relatively modest aid from Germany and other solvent European economies. When the dollar surged against nearly all other currencies in 2014 with no resulting inflation, the ideas of Krugman and his allies seemed to have prevailed.

Led by the dollar, floating paper currencies both outperformed gold and trumped the European experiment with many nation-states forced to adapt to a single standard of value. As Krugman argued, gold is simply a single standard applied to the world. Surely, Krugman said, citing Milton Friedman, the unitary gold standard would wreak global havoc like that inflicted by the unitary euro standard.[5]

So why do we push to end the current monetary regime? The reason is not irrational nostalgia for a misremembered "golden age." The reason is a decade and a half of economic failure so crippling and pervasive that it has led to a global revulsion against capitalism. Leading economists such as the former Treasury secretary Lawrence Summers and Robert Gordon of the National Bureau of Economic Research have concluded that the world's economies are entering an era of "secular stagnation," not merely a cyclical slowdown but a permanent decline of entrepreneurial innovation and technological advance.[6] Peter Thiel, by all odds the world's most visionary venture capitalist–philosopher, has declared that of four possibilities for the world economy—recurrent collapse, plateau, extinction, and technological takeoff—"the hardest one to imagine [is] accelerating takeoff toward a much better future."[7]

Deepening the global economic doldrums is a forced transfer of wealth from Main Street to Wall Street so gigantic that it has sharply skewed global measures of the distribution of wealth and income, bringing to a halt fifty years of miraculous and broad-based advances in global living standards. At the root of these catastrophes is a drastic abuse and debauch of money and banking led by U.S. and European megabanks.

The expansion of federal regulations and other laws has increased federal control of credit, skewing it away from technology and manufacturing and into real estate. The Basel process in Europe has extended these policies overseas.

In a hypertrophy of finance, an ever-increasing share of global profits has migrated to incestuous exchanges of liquidity by financial institutions transfixed by the oceanic movements of currency values. Trivializing banks, government policy has transformed them from a spearhead of investment in business to an obsequious role of borrowing money from the Fed at near-zero rates and lending it to the Treasury at rates as high as 2 percent, yielding a tidy risk free profit expandable through leverage protected by implicit and explicit government guarantees.

Intimidating the financial sector with constant litigation and addicted to fees and fines, regulators have turned banks into well-fed court eunuchs, periodically whipped and blandished and finally stultified. During the spurious expansion of the early 2000s, government policies, together with supportive litigation by nonprofits, pushed U.S. banks to bet the bulk of American investment capital on *housing*, essentially a consumption good already in oversupply. Banks and policy-makers then spread this error to Europe, pushing mortgage-backed securities on Irish, Spanish, and even German banks.

For these egregious errors, private and public, U.S. bankers collected *$2.2 trillion, mostly in bonuses* over a seven-year period.[8] Also profiteering on the crisis was Washington, which expanded regulations and controls under the amorphous Dodd-Frank blob of laws and even enriched housing subsidies under

Fannie Mae and Freddie Mac. In October 2014, as if nothing at all had been learned, the required down payments for taxpayer-guaranteed mortgages were dropped back down from a meager 5 percent to a risible 3 percent.

Meanwhile, as David Malpass has documented, crucial U.S. manufacturing and technology companies have been on a capital starvation diet since 2008 as private sector credit has shrunk as a share of GDP.[9]

Government money has shielded banks from many of the effects of these blunders and from mild but persistent consumer price index (CPI) inflation. But average American households have gone through an economic wringer with surging medical, education, food, utilities, and even—with ups and downs—fuel costs.[10] Doggedly opposed by the administration and the academy, fracking technology together with the strengthening dollar offer economic relief, but the damage has been done. The real incomes and net worth of the middle class have incurred a steady deterioration with falling labor hours, anemic employment growth, flat productivity, and the breakdown of families.

This persistent disaster would not have been possible without the concession by conservatives (with the delighted concurrence of liberals) that money is the one great exception to their general opposition to government monopoly—that among all the powers of the earth, only the power over money does not corrupt. Milton Friedman was wrong to think that control over the money supply empowers governments beneficently to stabilize its value. Instead, governments exploit their monetary control to steer money and credit away from productive enterprise and toward pet projects, political donors, and perverse policies.

This monetary coup, changing money from the medium of economic activity to the message itself, has thwarted economic growth, punished savers, and rewarded prestidigitory finance over innovation. Casting a shroud of uncertainty over all valuations, monetary manipulations shorten the time horizons of the economy. In information theory, the dominant science of our age, when a medium sends messages of its own—static on the line—it's called *noise*. Noise in the channel reduces the channel's capacity to transmit accurate information.

Obfuscating all economic activity, government money causes *inequitable* redistribution of wealth. Unlike mere inequality, these arbitrary government favors and privileges for producers of everything from ethanol and windmills to mortgage-backed securities and oceanic currency shuffles are actually destructive to the morale of capitalism and to the economic growth that fuels the opportunities of the middle class. This result is not surprising or even accidental. The actual purpose of both Keynesianism and monetarism, as well as every coin-clipping king or emperor in the history of the world, is to transform money, a measure of wealth, into wealth itself. It is driven by the delusionary dream that the government can create economic wealth for its rulers to spend. But changing the measuring stick has never improved the process of building economic value or anything else that has to work.

Chapter 6

Money in Information Theory

Surprise is the beginning of wisdom.

—David Gelernter

To grasp the fallacy of the reigning monetarist creed requires seeing that its baneful effects are not limited to inflation. The point about bad money is *not* that it converges with the worth of the paper it is printed on. It is worse than that. Falsifying the information basis of all prices, it stultifies entrepreneurs, deceives savers, and fosters tyranny.

Interest rates, for example, register the average expected returns across the economy. With a near-zero-interest-rate policy, the Fed falsely zeroes out the cost of time by nullifying the yield of saving. The Fed tells you that the opportunity cost of spending today is zero, which is true only if you die tomorrow. This deception retards economic growth. Rather than creating new assets, low-cost money borrowed from tomorrow bids up existing assets today. It produces no new learning or value and leaves no way to pay back the debt.

In the name of managing money, the Fed is trying to manipulate investors' time—their sense of present and future valuations. But time is not truly manipulable. It is an irreversible force impinging on every financial decision we make. The Fed policy merely confuses both savers and investors and contracts the horizons of investment, which in some influential trading strategies have shrunk to milliseconds.[1]

The critics of freely floating currencies have proposed two mostly complementary solutions: the creation of new currencies and the return to gold, the venerable historic standard monetary element. From the perspective of information theory, the two solutions converge. Each is an attempt to establish a regime of irreversibility—the assurance that transactions or contracts cannot be reversed, counterfeited, or nullified by private actors' double-dealing or by public entities' inflating the currency or countermanding contracts. The medium of exchange, standard of value, and store of wealth cannot be subject to arbitrary change from outside.

Irreversibility is a function of time. Government control of the distribution of money and credit gives rise to endless opportunities to rerun the race against time in a way that the government's favorite children always win. The principal attraction of both gold and recent experiments in digital money is precisely that they give us money as irreversible as time itself.

The second law of thermodynamics ordains that entropy as disorder always increases and cannot be reversed. You cannot reconstruct an egg from an omelet or reuse the energy that heated your house or that flowed kinetically over Niagara Falls. It is entropy that imposes an irreversible arrow of time on the physical world. Thermodynamics runs one way, irreversibly, and defines the essence of time.

Sound money requires hostility to time travel. You do not want someone to go back and re-spend the same money that he has already given you or reverse the transactions that you have made. You do not want your customers to bounce their checks or your bank or the government to bounce yours. Sound money is the equivalent of scientific integrity: the system must not permit the manipulation of data after the experiment has taken place.

Gold achieves irreversibility through its refractory chemistry and the time-based entropy of extraction. As master of the mint in eighteenth-century England, Isaac Newton spent much of his time proving that gold could not be hacked, counterfeited, or reverse-engineered from other elements.[2] As Nick Gillespie of *Reason* magazine has observed, Newton was not an alchemist so much as an "anti-alchemist."[3] Bitcoin and other digital currencies offer similar irreversibility through complex mathematics and software using a time-stamped public "blockchain" of transactions. Latter-day Newtons are constantly trying to hack bitcoin.

Gold and bitcoin both protect the measuring stick from the advance of physical capital or technology and even the learning curves of labor. A metric cannot be part of what it measures. If the measuring stick changes in response to economic progress, it cannot measure that progress. In order to bear creative changes it must not change itself. To be a gauge that is exempt from the turmoil of markets, it must be rooted outside those markets. It must somehow cancel capital, technology, and learning. Like the electromagnetic spectrum, which bears all the messages of the

Internet to and from your smartphone or computer, it must be rooted in the absolute speed of light, the ultimate guarantor of the integrity of time.

Dominating our own era and revealing in fundamental ways the nature of money is the information theory of Kurt Gödel, John von Neumann, Alan Turing, and Claude Shannon. Information theory tells us that information is not order but disorder, not the predictable regularity that contains no news, but the unexpected modulation, the surprising bits. But human creativity and surprise depend upon a matrix of regularities, from the laws of physics to the stability of money.[4]

Information theory has impelled the global ascendancy of information technology. From worldwide webs of glass and light to a boom in biotech based on treating life itself as chiefly an information system, a new system of the world is transforming our lives. Its roots are not in the necessary carriers of predictable physics and chemistry but in the creativity and disorder at higher levels of the hierarchy of life. Information theory operates on the epistemic plane where human beings conduct falsifiable experiments that yield learning and accumulate knowledge.

The lesson of information theory is that irreversible money cannot be the measure of itself, defined by the values it gauges. It is part of a logical system, and like all such systems it must be based on values outside itself. It must be rooted in the entropy of irreversible time.

When the bitcoin innovators Satoshi Nakamoto and Nick Szabo sought to invent new forms of money, they explicitly designed algorithms that nullified the effects of technological advance in computer technology. As Moore's Law improves the computer systems used to validate transactions and integrate them with the bitcoin blockchain, for example, the "proof of work" challenge in the algorithm becomes proportionately more difficult and the reward smaller.

Bitcoin "miners" could gain their specified rewards, but they could not use their superfast devices to accelerate their own transactions or capture greater personal returns from them. Regardless of the evolution of computer technology, every group of transactions in the blockchain and every new issue of bitcoins would require a ten-minute span to verify and integrate, mine and mint. Devoid of the outside influences of capital and technology, the source of bitcoin value becomes the pure irreversible passage of time.

The bitcoin theorists based this principle on the immemorial experience of gold. Largely by happenstance, gold has mostly canceled capital and technology. As mining and extraction technology have improved, the exhaustion of the "easy" nuggets near the surface has required probing on to ever deeper and more difficult lodes and more attenuated deposits. Throughout history, with few contrary episodes such as the discovery of the Potosi bonanza in Peru in the seventeenth century, the increasing difficulty of mining new, deeper gold has nullified all advances in the technology of mining. As a result, gold has served as a gauge, perdurable and pure, of the time consumed in extracting it.

Gold is the most monetary of elements because its cost is most closely tied to the time entailed in its extraction. All the some 170,000 metric tons of gold that have accumulated through the centuries is still available today. Virtually all the world's gold reserves are known. This available supply dominates the price. At the margin, gold's value is determined by hours alone, not labor plus capital.

Today it costs close to $1,200 to mine a new ounce of gold, which sells for about the same amount. As Kwasi Kwarteng has shown, throughout history to the present day, the value of the world's available gold stock has almost always tracked the value of the world's GDP, remaining close to 10 percent.[5]

Despite technological advances and population growth, the stock of gold rises every year, never falls, and has averaged 2.5 percent annual growth for centuries.[6] Gold thus has been the only commodity whose future price is always equal to the spot price plus the rate of interest over the time period. A million paper dollars held since 1913, when the Federal Reserve Bank was created, would be worth $20,000 today, down 98 percent. A million dollars of gold in 1913 would now be worth $62 million.[7] Aligned with irreversible time, gold is the monetary element that holds value rather than dissipates it.

Many food and housing prices are set by the cost of time and labor. If gold's value is constant, then all other prices can become variables around that constant. Just as the North Star provides a fixed reference for celestial navigation and astronomy, so gold provides a fixed reference for the value of the galaxy of goods and services.[8] Breaking the link of the dollar to gold broke the link to time, devalued labor, and is at the root of the decline in the middle class in America.

When the tie to gold ended in 1971, governments pushed real estate as a haven from dollar depreciation, turning the U.S. economy from an industrial powerhouse into a financial and consumption casino.

Contrast this cancelation of capital in gold and bitcoin with the system of international currency trading that dominates contemporary money. Now at $5.3 trillion per day, currency trading dwarfs all the globe's stock markets and is seventy-three times greater than all trade in goods and services.[9] To deal with the floods of monetary change, banks spend half a trillion dollars on information technology, decisively leading all other sectors in computer outlays.[10] The work of maintaining the measuring stick now costs 20 percent more in computer equipment than all the world's information technology for manufacturing new goods. Moreover, that work yields a volatile but steadily rising proportion of all banking profits.

In other words, our current floating-rate system fails to cancel capital, technology, and learning. Instead capital, technology, entrepreneurial ingenuity, and government power together largely determine the earnings in the financial system. In a form of private seigniorage the profits from creating money—the largest traders capture hundreds of billions of dollars or dollar equivalents every year from setting the measuring stick. Therefore, it is not a measuring stick at all but a speculative ocean of currencies that banks surf for profits. In what looks uncomfortably like a protection racket, the banks extract these profits as a kind of volatility tax on the companies that use them to hedge currencies.

Moving toward a modern gold standard, complemented by a bitcoin or other Internet digital currency standard, would eliminate all this profitable froth. Under a gold standard, trading imbalances are nearly meaningless. Flowing freely to redress any imbalance, capital is more mobile than goods and services and can determine the balance of trade. Under the gold standard, the world enjoyed some two centuries of ever-expanding global trade and investment without any semblance of balance on the current account. Americans, for example, ran trade deficits year in year out for two hundred years while rising to a century of dominance in the world economy.[11] If the United States returns to stable money, rooted in time, the twenty-first century can be an American century as well.

But to fully understand money, we should consider the philosophy behind the most radical experiment in digital money.

Chapter 7

What Bitcoin
Can Teach

*Bitcoin…is the perfect form of money for the Internet
because it is fast, secure, and borderless…. Essentially, bitcoin
mining decentralizes the currency-issuance and clearing functions of a central bank…. [It] has ushered in a wave of innovation in currencies, financial services, economics, distributed
systems, voting systems, corporate governance, and contracts.*

—Andreas Antonopoulos, *Mastering Bitcoin* (2015)

Today the established theories of top-down money face serious challenges from digital alternatives on the Internet and
from the perennial appeal of the case for gold. Both of these
forms of money offer escape from the centralized regime of monetarism. Both offer monetary systems that affirm Friedman's
cogent theories of freedom rather than his erroneous ideas of
control.

Gold has been ascendant in Asia, which has become the new
spearhead of world economic growth and capitalism, with tax
rates generally between one-half and one-third of those in the
West.[1]

Meanwhile, around the globe, transactions are shifting
toward the Internet. Although online purchases remain between
6 and 7 percent of all commerce, Internet trade is expanding

rapidly.[2] On the Internet, technological change accelerates, digital currencies like bitcoin and its imitators are gaining ground, and impatience mounts with the prevailing mazes of bureaucratic moneys, fees, finagles, security rigmaroles, defaults, and escrows.

To buy something on the Internet, you often have to give the supplier sufficient information—credit card number, expiration date, address, security code, mother's maiden name, and so on—to defraud you or even to usurp your identity. This information therefore has to be protected at high cost in firewalled central repositories and private networks, which are irresistible targets for hackers.

With transactional overhead dominated by offline financial infrastructure, micropayments are uneconomic, and the Internet fills with mendacious free goods, bogus contracts, and pop-up hustles. Some 36 percent of web pages are spurious, emitted by bots to snare information from unwary surfers.[3] At the same time, Silicon Valley moves toward an "internet of things," sensors and devices—from heart monitors and "smart grid" gauges to automated cars and heating systems—linked across the net and needing secure automated transactions without offline intermediaries. Reform of world money is less a far-fetched dream than a rising imperative. Gold and digital currencies converge to provide a new solution to the enigma of money. Although there are many potential rivals, bitcoin is the most complete and tested form of digital currency that does not require centralized management. Rooted in time, it shares the stability of value that has made gold the quintessential monetary element.

To the Internet, bitcoin introduces an acutely needed new security model based not on privacy but on publicity. Privacy just invites hacking of the central repositories that provide it and the supposedly secure networks that protect it. Bitcoin is a public ledger of transactions that cannot be abused or manipulated or falsified, because it is published on potentially millions of computers around the world.

The bitcoin ledger uses mathematical hashing tools to incorporate in every new transaction identifiable time-stamped traces of every previous transaction ever conducted in bitcoin since the "Genesis block" in 2009. Because each new block of transactions bears a mathematical fingerprint of all previous blocks, it cannot be changed without changing all the blocks. Because each transaction is verified and propagated to all the computers on the network, it cannot be reversed or changed without hacking a majority of all the computers on the network.

Making the revelation of personal information unnecessary, bitcoin can be used on any network, however insecure. On top of the existing convention of seven layers of Internet infrastructure, it builds a new layer of functionality—a layer 8—just as the hypertext transfer protocol (http) builds on the transmission control protocol/Internet protocol (TCP/IP) network layer. This new transactions layer allows for the separation of the security and identification functions from the network. Based on new breakthroughs in information theory, security can be *heterarchical* rather than hierarchical—distributed on millions of provably safe devices beyond the network and unreachable from it. It is a security paradigm diametrically opposed to the existing morass of passwords, user names, PINs, personal tokens, and post-hack fixes on the network.

In a bitcoin transaction, there is no more need for the disclosure of personal information than in a cash transaction. With no personal information transferred—but all such information preserved—there is no need to restrict the transaction to protected networks, encrypted "Swift" banking transfer lines, or ATM networks. Wi-Fi or Bluetooth or your cellphone link suffices. Names and passwords and other authentication details do not need to be stored. An effort to hack one of the computers and change the blockchain ledger would be pointless, as the correct ledger would exist on myriad other computers.

Gold, however, remains the leading player. In fact, bitcoin's mysterious, pseudonymous founder, one "Satoshi Nakamoto," specifically mimicked gold in developing his digital money, which becomes more difficult to "mine" with the passage of time. Its value, like gold's, is ultimately based on its scarcity. It is not a competitor with gold but an Internet money that simulates the properties of the monetary metal and offers a path toward a gold-inspired standard for the net.

Understanding any kind of money still requires coming to terms with the meaning of gold. In the new information theory of money, the crucial clue turns out to be the deeper significance of Friedman's error: the role of velocity.

The most sophisticated writing on money today has come out of the research on digital currency and cryptology that engendered bitcoin. In the ten years before bitcoin's launch in January 1999, Nakamoto expounded his thinking in thousands of posts on cryptographic bulletin boards on the net. In order to develop bitcoin, this movement first mastered and then transformed the theory of gold. In the process, it cast new and penetrating light on the importance of velocity and time.

The leading philosopher of the movement is Nick Szabo, who named his first proposal for a digital currency "bitgold." A shrewd analyst and historian of the evolution of money, Szabo in the

1990s threw a wrench into the Drexlerian nanotech movement, with its dream of building new molecules from scratch using nano-replicators, offering a prize to anyone who could create a *macro*-replicator out of Lego blocks or other toy-like potential replicators. If you can't build a macro-replicator, you probably cannot build one with nano-pincers and electron microscopes.[4] There was no one to claim the prize. Since then Szabo has been focusing on the easier enigmas of money and gold.

Though he denies it, Szabo has long been suspected of being Satoshi Nakamoto, and several analyses have shown his prose above all others to conform to the idiosyncrasies of Nakamoto's bitcoin paper. Known in the early 1990s for his canny ruminations on strategies for network anonymity and pseudonymity, Szabo now writes a pithy, original, and very occasional blog on money matters called *Unenumerated*[5] but is otherwise scarcely or skittishly represented on the Internet.

According to Szabo, money succeeds not because it can capture all the dimensions of multifaceted value but because it obviates the need for such impossible calculations. Although much free-market thinking holds that money measures the value of goods, that assumption is simplistic. The value of goods can far exceed their price. Much of the value in an economy comes from what economists call "consumer surplus"—the difference between what we actually pay and what we might have been willing to pay.

Money can never be an accurate gauge of the intrinsic worth of goods and services. It facilitates exchange. Any way of freeing an economy from preplanned barter is an enormous benefit. "Measuring something that actually indicates value is hard.... Measuring something that is related to value and immune to spoofing is hardest of all," writes Szabo. "To create anything of value requires some sacrifice.... Since, ... absent a perfect exchange market of globally optimized barter, [we can't] directly measure the value of something, we may be able to estimate it indirectly by measuring something else."

That something else, Szabo saw, is *time:* "Time measures *input* rather than *output*...sacrifice, rather than results." Szabo understood that the recognition of money as time freed the slaves. The invention of reliable and recognizable timepieces—clocks and bell towers—liberated workers from the bondage of piecework, which entails regimentation to count the pieces and favors quantity over quality, slavery over free labor.

Time as money is a crucial insight behind the value of gold and the creation of bitcoin as a form of digital gold. But the theory is incomplete without an understanding of velocity. According to Szabo, velocity is the critical element differentiating money from commodities. Over the course of human history, various commodities evolved from mere consumables into collectibles and thence into wearable décor and jewelry. On occasion, in a phase change, beads made out of clam shells became "wampum." Thus we "shell out clams" to buy things. As Szabo explains, that change into money occurs when the value of a thing as a medium for transactions eclipses its value as a collectible, or as Szabo puts it, when it increases "the ratio of velocity to current value." He points to the history of New Amsterdam (as New York was originally known), where a seventeenth-century Dutch entrepreneur had his bank arrange a large debt in wampum. The Indian baubles had crossed the velocity barrier to become a vessel for indirect transactions— real money.

Many people believe that money must begin as a commodity like wampum or gold and then evolve into a transactions medium. But once wampum became money, Szabo argues, its role as jewelry was eclipsed, becoming as irrelevant as gold jewelry is irrelevant to gold money. Money is not something else. It is not a commodity. It is intrinsically a unitary measure of value.

Many critics thought Nakamoto had ruined the system by refusing to guarantee results. They wanted his computational puzzles as a "proof of work" to verify transactions also to accomplish "good works." They wanted bitcoin's computations to calculate complex protein folds for cancer therapy or to do search for extraterrestrial intelligence (SETI) calculations for the discovery of other intelligent beings in space or to fathom intricate feedback loops in the models of global warming. But a measuring stick cannot be part of what it measures. A currency generates value by measuring value. If what it is doing is already deemed valuable, money becomes just another self-referential loop, where elites define what should be deemed important.

Gold is money not because it is shiny and beautiful but because it has the properties of a transactions medium necessary to achieve take-off speed as money. As Richard Vigilante of Whitebox Advisors observes with Chestertonian aplomb, "Money is not valuable because it is really jewelry; jewelry is valuable because it is really money."[6]

Money is a matter of velocity—the turnover rate of the transactional media. Its value as a transactional medium must exceed its value for other uses or it can never become money. It functions in the frequency domain and can be measured there, with its velocity and amplitude. The power of monetary investments rises by the square of the amplitude of the learning curve they launch.

Szabo's basic point is the same one I contested with Friedman in China. In economics, velocity rules. In moral terms, velocity equals our freedom. We rule, as we learn.

Chapter 8

Where "Hayeks" Go Wrong

From Italy's financial community arises a different critique of prevailing moneys, one that applies not only to fiat currencies like the dollar and the euro, but also to gold and its digital imitators. Let us take this critique seriously and see what we learn about it using our new information theory of money.

Ferdinando Ametrano has seen currencies come and go. He can look the dollar in the face and detect Botox in its apparently smooth Ben Franklin jowls. A self-described "fat, short, bald, and ugly" nerd in his forties, with red eyeglass frames and fashionable bristles, Ametrano began as a physicist. Like so many "quants," he is a master of the interplay of math and matter. In 2010 he invented the open-source QuantLib framework for monetary math. As he describes it, "QuantLib is a free, open-source quantitative finance C++ library for modeling, pricing, trading, and risk management in real-life."[1] Derivatives traders use it around the world to guide their decisions.

Sounding like Steve Forbes, Ametrano stresses, "When the value of money changes...it is not just the value of one good that is changing, but the unit against which every other good is measured." He warns, "If high inflation is money's heart attack, persistent deflation is money's cancer."[2] Both gold and bitcoin, he declared, show a fatal deflationary bias.

"In the last twenty years," Ametrano points out, "it has become more and more clear that the banking system built around fiat currencies is not adequate to the new digital realm defined by mobile communication, Internet, and social networks.... As everybody gets used to carrying around in their mobile phones powerful computers, hours of video and audio entertainment, and immediate access to an immense amount of information, the expectation has arisen to be able to pocket a whole efficient and fair monetary, financial, and banking system along with it."[3]

Yet, in his view, gold and digital gold cannot play this role because of their deflationary bias. To back up his critique, Ametrano summons Friedrich Hayek. The eminent Austrian offered similar objections to a proposal for private money backed by gold: "It would turn out to be a very good investment, for the reason that because of the increased demand for gold the value of gold would go up; but that very fact would make it very unsuitable as money."[4]

Ametrano adds, "The unfeasibility of a bitcoin [or gold] loan is similar to that of a bitcoin or [gold] salary: neither a borrower nor an employer would want to face the risk of seeing her debt or salary liabilities growing a hundredfold in a few years."[5] He concludes, "This is the cryptocurrency paradox: In the successful attempt to get rid of any centralized monetary authority using the Bitcoin protocol, the bitcoin currency has inadvertently thrown away the flexibility of an elastic monetary policy."

In a presentation to the Bank of Italy, Ametrano rejected the idea that bitcoin will lose its instability with wider adoption: "This is indeed true, but not at all sufficient for stable prices, as demonstrated by the need of monetary actions to stabilize even globally accepted currencies such as the Euro and US dollar."[6]

One can imagine the eminent men of Banca d'Italia nodding solemnly at this observation. But Ametrano is a devout Hayekian and does not like arbitrary policy from central banks any more than he likes arbitrary deflation from a distributed peer-to-peer currency.

As an alternative, Ametrano presents the idea of a new kind of coin that he dubs "Hayek money." Let's call them "hayeks." These coins overcome the putative volatility of gold or bitcoin as units of account by continually rebasing the value in response to changes in a commodity index. He would have all the wallets in the digital coin system regularly increment or decrement the number of units in accord with the movement of the index. If you had fifty hayeks when the index was at one hundred, you would have one hundred hayeks when the index went to two hundred.

In response to objections that these quantitative changes in individual wallets are alarmingly novel and unorthodox, the Italian guru points out that central banks now do the same thing. They routinely manipulate their own digital wallet—the "monetary base"—by expanding it during deflation and reducing it during inflation. As Ametrano observes, these actions of the central bank affect all the holders of the currency, depleting the accounts of debtors during contractions or of creditors during inflations.

As the Austrian school of economics explains, these actions also impart immediate benefits to the banking institutions that carry them out, affording them the profits of seigniorage, gains stemming from the difference between the coin's cost of production and its value. The central banks and government Treasuries win most of these gains. But these quantitative changes also lavishly benefit any early borrowers or lenders of the government money who can act before related price changes propagate through the economy.

Central banks currently change the money supply through a Rube Goldberg contrivance of open-market operations buying and selling Treasury notes, "quantitative easing" through purchase of private bonds and other assets, adaptive "twists" of yield curves and maturities, reserve requirements regulating bank leverage, and interest-rate manipulations that change the cost of money.

These measures deny most of the users of the money any pro rata increase in their quantities during inflations and inflict borrowers with the full brunt of contractionary policy (they have to pay back their loans with more valuable units than they received). In the late 1990s, an unexpected 26 percent deflation (increase in the dollar's value) bankrupted a thousand companies that had incurred large debts in the multifaceted process of building out the Internet with advanced fiber optics.[7]

By contrast, Hayek money would automatically expand or shrink the money supply in an entirely equitable and proportionate way, distributing these changes across the entire range of coin holders, with no preference for cronies, or affiliated banks, or other special interests.

Hayek money is the proposal of a libertarian. Hayek is the cynosure of libertarians, and he wished currency to become market-based. Escaping the distortions of monopoly and sovereignty, management of hayeks could rely on an automatic formula. If it didn't work well, other entities would launch competitive currencies. Hayeks might return the world to the Edenic realm of "free banking" of the nineteenth century. Free banking might have failed as the country was unified by railroads and telegraphs. But today it may well become possible again on the Internet.

Hayek money is the proposal of a banker, who believes in the power of monetary policy. And Ametrano's system would be based on the analysis of an economist, who believes in the validity of price indices.

The issuance of new coins would be governed by the change in the prices of a basket of commodities comprising precious metals, such as gold and silver; standard foodstuffs, such as wheat and soy; and energy units, such as "Brent crude oil" and natural gas. All these items benefit from their relatively immutable unit definitions. Whether troy ounces of gold or British thermal units of energy or standard bushels of wheat, these items—so it is maintained—have not changed in character or essential quality for a century.

An economist with a specialty in quantification, "a quant," Ametrano also believes that the appropriate index could be modulated by inclusion of other relatively scientific price-level indices such as the general inflation corrective, the Federal Reserve's GDP deflator. Also available are the personal consumption expenditures inflation indicator of the Department of Commerce and the consumer and producer price indices (CPI and PPI) tracked by the Department of Labor. As the Fed explains, the most common type of inflation measure "excludes items that tend to go up and down in price dramatically or often, like food and energy items." For these, "a large price change in one period does not necessarily tend to be followed by another large change in the same direction in the following period.... Core inflation measures that leave out items with volatile prices can be useful in assessing inflation trends."[8]

Ametrano's excellent paper incorporates, with stark lucidity, the fundamental weaknesses of the prevailing theories of money. They are all trying to find some stable proxy in the real world to "peg" to. "Two families of Hayek monies" might peg to different commodities, writes Ametrano: "Gold, as the immemorial monetary element," and "petroleums, grains and industrial metals." But we already know of Ametrano's and Hayck's ambivalence about gold, and "petroleums, grains and industrial metals" show more volatility. After all, grains and petroleums are precisely the items that tend to be excluded from "core inflation."

Thus hayeks would move the focus of monetary policy from quantitative changes to changes in the composition of the commodity index. That is already happening in the world of the dollar, with "hedonic" adjustments and other technical adaptations of the CPI. It takes armies of accountant-economists, in several branches of the U.S. government and similar entities at the Organisation for Economic Co-operation and Development, the United Nations, the World Bank, and other institutions, to track all the price movements in the market. Pursuing the calculation of "purchasing power parity," they try to gauge which changes signify the "real" level of prices. MIT includes literally millions of prices around the world in its comprehensive index called "Beta."

Giving up on all these perplexities, the *Economist* sometimes throws up its hands and resolves on a global "Big Mac" index. Others prefer a "Brooks Brothers Index" tying the price of a business suit to an ounce of gold.[9]

Under the "hayek" regime, the management of the basket on which all valuations and arbitrage will rely becomes all-important. The central question in political economy would then become the procedure and timing of basket management. We already know that Ametrano (and putatively Hayek) have impugned gold in this role because of its deflationary bias. Ametrano proposes a commodity price index determined with a "resilient consensus process that does not rely on central third party authorities." He seems to prefer an index heavily influenced by the prices of grains and Brent crude oil and makes an effort to show that such an index would result in relatively stable prices.

Ametrano quotes Hayek: "Changes in the importance of the commodities, the volume in which they were traded, and the relative stability or sensitivity of their prices (especially the degree to which they were determined competitively or not) might suggest alterations to make the currency more popular."[10] An extreme example, says Ametrano, "would be a major breakthrough in green energy that would make petroleum useless." So much for Brent crude.

What Ametrano sees as an exotic possible breakthrough in energy technology, however, is in fact the condition of the entire entrepreneurial economy. All existing goods and services are vulnerable to innovation, which is, as Joseph Schumpeter insisted, the very law of capitalism. To treat it as some kind of exceptional or anomalous event is a fundamental error.

The information theory of capitalism defines growth as *learning*. Its microeconomic manifestation is the learning or experience curve in individual businesses and industries. As we saw in chapter 2, it is the most thoroughly documented phenomenon in all enterprise, ordaining that the cost of producing any good or service drops by between 20 percent and 30 percent with every doubling of total units sold.

Crucially, the curve extends to customers, who learn how to use the product and multiply applications as it drops in price. The proliferation of hundreds of thousands of applications for Apple's iPhones, for example, represented the learning curve of the users as much as the learning curve at Apple.

All these curves document the essential identity of growth and learning as a central rule of capitalist change. Sound management of money cannot focus on finding stable elements among existing goods and services that are endlessly multifarious and changing. These very changes are what money must measure. The only feasible goal of policy is to foster neutrality between the past and the future. This entails equity not between industries or localities but chronological equity: equity not in space but in time.

What Ametrano is advocating, with all the confidence of his expertise, is submission of monetary policy to the interests of the most-static and stagnant interests in the economy—the very parts that have passed beyond their learning curves onto a plateau of drifting costs defended by expanded political lobbies. This is what "commodities" are. It is rearview-mirror monetary policy reflecting the need of recumbent sectors for protection against more-creative domestic and foreign rivals.

By seeking to impart a bias of inflation to prices, the commodity basket tends to a zero-sum vision that fosters trade wars of devaluation. The basket of commodities is the one part of the economy that operates as a zero-sum game. As it erodes through the advance of innovation, its prices tend to drift upward, skewing the time value of money.

The redemptive force of gold is its neutrality in time and thus its orientation toward the future. Hayeks would substitute an anachronistic commodity basket for a predictable deflation based on the scarcity of time and abundance of learning.

Commodities are by definition low entropy, but if all valuation and arbitrage is based on them, politics will converge on the basket and its composition. What is the composition of a representative basket of goods? It is the backward-looking selection of products that were important in the existing economic configuration. It is a representation of the economy of the past, consisting of mature products and ingredients. These are goods that have already attained volumes that put them beyond the fast-moving parts of their learning curves. As the key element in a monetary index, commodities impart an inflationary bias to economies, penalizing the future, rewarding borrowers, and punishing investors.

The genius of gold is not to root valuation in some politicized process of sampling the past, but to root it in the residual scarcities in a capitalist economy of abundance. The deflationary bias reflects the reality of a capitalist economy of abundance and creativity playing out against the irreversible passage of time.

To the Austrian economics of subjectivity, time provides an objective foundation. In reaching for commodities in which to anchor his system of value, Ametrano should have ended with gold, with its intimate links to the irreversibility of time. In the end, a test of bitcoin or any other blockchain will be the price of gold. If in a mature bitcoin system the gold chain massively bifurcates from the blockchain, it will signify a disorientation of values. As in bitcoin itself, the majority of users will decide which branch bears economic truth.[11]

Since its creation in 2009, bitcoin's price movements have been 80.4 percent correlated with the gold price.[12] Bitcoin's relatively tiny float has imparted much greater volatility. But its following gold down in 2014 should not have been alarming. If and when bitcoin matures into a meaningful currency, its kinship with gold, rooted in *time*, should become increasingly manifest.

The conservative theories of money fail to address these issues. Let us now turn to the premier money theorists on the Left and see what they get right and wrong.

Chapter 9

The Piketty-Turner Thesis

*Egalitarians never seem to understand that promoting
economic equality in theory means promoting resent-
ments and polarization in practice, making everyone
worse off.*

—Thomas Sowell (2016)

The Left is right: current policies are exacerbating what it
calls "inequality," unjustly rewarding nonproductive
wealth. When Manhattan flats go through the roof,
nobody has learned anything but how to turn his home into an
ATM for as long as the boom lasts. Wall Street and Washington
working together are forcing Silicon Valley to play the unicorn
game and Main Street to face foreclosure and stagnation.

Where the Left goes wrong is in diagnosing the cause and
therefore understanding the cure. Across the Atlantic, in France
and the United Kingdom, influential people have noticed the
hypertrophy of finance and called for a new economic theory.
Several candidates offer policy breakthroughs intended to be as
far reaching as the New Deal that supposedly ended the Great
Depression.

We have already met the Frenchman Thomas Piketty, that cherubic scourge of wealth, bearing credentials from Harvard and MIT, electrifying the crowds with *Capital in the Twenty-First Century* and its new "laws of capitalism."[1] Piketty warns that a society that stops growing will grow fat on finance and real estate. The accumulated overhang of capital and inheritance will overwhelm the future as entrepreneurs become mere rentiers of old wealth.

From the early 1970s to the 2000s, as economic growth declined, financial obesity became increasingly evident. Combined financial assets and liabilities in advanced economies rose from levels of four or five times national income to today's level of ten to fifteen times national income in the United States, Japan, and France and twenty times national income in the United Kingdom, the world financial center. Following Piketty's paradigm faithfully, accompanying this tumescence of finance—the harvest of what I call "hypertrophy"[2]—was sluggish growth and increased inequality.

Piketty might be surprised to find that many American conservatives agree with his analysis. If growth collapses and money expands, the financial and real estate sectors of the economy will swell. Such an economy will find many avid critics on all sides of the political spectrum.

Following in Piketty's footsteps is Lord Adair Turner, who in 2008, at the height of the financial crisis, became the chairman of the Financial Services Authority, which regulates British banks. In 2015 he assumed the chairmanship of London's Institute for New Economic Thinking (INET) and surpassed Piketty with a compelling tract, *Between Debt and the Devil*, based on the same trends and similar formulae.[3] Both Piketty and Turner align themselves with the thinking of the American Nobel laureates Paul Krugman and Joseph Stiglitz, who contend that "the price of inequality" is slow growth and secular stagnation.[4] They have that backward: inevitable effects of government policies that guarantee secular stagnation are inequality and the unjust enrichment of the already well-to-do, who can afford to buy influence and preference from the state.

Brooding over this hothouse efflorescence of "new economic thinking" is George Soros, the cerebral billionaire and disciple (from the left) of the philosopher Karl Popper. (From the right, I uphold Popperian empiricism as a key reason for the epistemic success of capitalism.) Soros expounds a theory of "market reflexivity," according to which economic results stem less from fixed "facts" and fundamentals than from the interplay of investors' opinions and strategies, which, in complex feedback loops, determine the facts and fundamentals.[5] As a currency trader supreme, Soros is accurately describing the market that he has mastered. Partly bankrolling both Piketty's and Turner's work, Soros cofounded INET and has lauded *Between Debt and the Devil* as "the most penetrating analysis...to appear since the crash of 2008." I may even agree with him on that.

In an unusual Right-Left consensus on our economic predicament, Turner reaches most of the same conclusions that Piketty does. Documenting the hypertrophy of finance, Turner's book begins, "For many decades before the 2007–2008 crisis, finance got bigger relative to the real economy. Its share of the U.S. and UK economies tripled between 1950 and the 2000s. Stock-market turnover increased dramatically as a percentage of GDP. On average across advanced economies private-sector debt increased from 50 percent of national income in 1950 to

170 percent in 2006.... From 1980 on, the growth was turbo-charged by the financial innovations of securitization and derivatives; by 2008 there were $400 trillion of derivative contracts outstanding."[6]

Like Piketty, Turner invokes the insights of Henry George, who more than a century ago described in *Progress and Poverty* the tendency of wealth to congeal around scarce urban acreage.[7] Drilling in on the fundamental problem, Turner asserts, "At the core of financial instability lies the interaction between the potentially limitless supply of bank credit and the highly inelastic supply of real estate and locationally specific land.... [R]ising real estate and land prices have been the predominant and inevitable driver of the increase in wealth-to-income ratios that Thomas Piketty has documented.... Credit and real estate price cycles, as a result, have been not just part of the story of financial instability [and inequality]...they are close to the whole story."[8]

As an explanation for the current migration of money to real estate, Turner cites the radical low capital-intensity of "winner-take-all" information and communications technologies. With a near-zero marginal cost of production of new units of software or bandwidth, relatively small investments of capital yield ever-higher returns. The persons earning this bounty tend to invest it in the only large available sector that can absorb this money, namely real estate. In addition, Turner and Piketty contend, investment in scarce real estate is a function of increasing wealth and is thus both a source and a result of increasing inequality.

Real estate is also central to the net worth of the middle class. The Great Recession was made possible by the mobilization of most of the governments and associated banks of East and West in a mad rush to pump money into securitized mortgages on the margins of the middle class and below. Inequality in a top-heavy, slow-growing economy inspired a drive to substitute credit for real income and wealth. The result was a huge overhang of debt in the middle class and a swelling of assets at the top.

As a remedy for these disorders, Piketty would impose a progressive annual tax on capital. By a static analysis, such a tax might reduce the yield of capital to the rate of GDP expansion and thus eliminate the bias toward top-heavy accumulation by elites. Upholding the secular stagnation theory of permanent growth slowdown, he naturally focuses on depressing the return to capital. Taking money from the rich and giving it to government might seem to address "inequality." But by putting capital into the hands of the least productive users of it—politicians—he would aggravate the very stagnation he warns against.

Turner and Piketty both urge an array of global wealth taxes as high as 10 percent and new marginal income-tax rates as high as 80 percent. They also call for new regulatory regimes for alternative energy and new capital controls. Turner advocates 30 to 40 percent reserve requirements for banks, regulations on "shadow banking" derivatives and securities, restrictions on international capital movements, and a global regime of trade rules. Since they believe the Great Recession had many causes, they marshal many regulatory tools to combat it and prevent its recurrence. Because they diagnose the problem as "inequality" rather than "stagnation," they propose mechanical and accounting solutions that do not address what real people care about and what affects our well-being: opportunity, creativity, and growth.

Reflecting an accountant-economist's vision of global equilibrium, this regulatory regime would in effect require every country to maintain a balance between production and consumption, imports and exports. No major export-led growth would be permitted in emerging nations like China, no specialization in venture capital and investment in advanced economies, no exemption from the worldwide web of welfare safety nets that spur consumption, no inequality in the winner-take-all global technology race, and no flow of investment capital to low-tax regimes, or real estate sumps.

Unlike Piketty, Turner spurns "secular stagnation." He wants the world economy to return to the higher economic growth rates of the past, and he thinks he knows how it can be done. But Turner's mistake is to assume, as some conservative monetarists do, that the government manipulation of monopoly money is a key to economic growth. A devout believer in the power of money, Turner wants central banks to counteract the existing overhang of private credit with the issuance of new money in any volumes needed to maintain "adequate levels of nominal demand." Within an overall regime of inflation controls and cautions, Turner believes, government money creation is more favorable to growth than is private money creation through fractional reserve banking.

To Turner, money creation is a boundless abundance ("a potentially limitless supply," to quote Milton Friedman), whether the credit is created by private banks or "printed" by the central bank. Turner prefers central bank money because it can be steered away from real estate and other existing assets into new assets. He favors government infrastructure, education, healthcare, technology, and other public benefits. In the quest for increased nominal demand, central banks can always create deposits at will and over the course of time can provide any needed amount. Inflation seems a remote threat in an epoch of near-zero interest rates and collapsing commodity prices.

Nonetheless, Turner correctly warns that real estate by its very nature is scarce. If the private banking system were permitted to generate credit at will, it would flow toward urban land, the price of which would be bid up vertiginously in the overflow of wealth from the new information economy. He shares the skepticism of Austrian economists about fractional reserve banking, whereby financial institutions can multiply deposits into cataracts of money and debt. Thus he prefers high reserve requirements and restrictions on international capital flows.

What insight does our new information theory of money give us into these prescriptions? In the new theory, the Turner-Piketty thesis rests on the triad of infinite time, finite space, and infinite information. As proxies for the finitude of space, choice urban and agricultural land absorbs excess demand stemming from the limitless expandability of the money supply.

The indefinite expansion of the money supply, however, is possible only to the degree money is freed from the constraints of time under a zero-interest-rate policy. Without any reliable metric or constraint, the nominal "money supply" can indeed serve as an inescapable abundance. But real money, whether gold or its digital equivalents, is founded on the scarcity of time. Time in practice is always finite, and money that reflects that finitude will limit the spiral of bidding for existing assets such as real estate. Mind—knowledge and information—may be ultimately infinite, as boundless as imagination, but in practice human creativity is bounded by time (money).

Although Turner believes that the remedy for capitalist excesses is strict and relentless regulation, the current excesses spring from regulations on all sides. Fostering runaway credit are banks and other financial institutions with government guarantees under

Dodd-Frank, access to central bank discount windows, federal deposit insurance, and limited liability. Then the rules push banks toward real estate through near-zero interest rates on debt, through guarantees from Fannie Mae, Freddie Mac, and the Federal Housing Administration, through insurance from the Federal Deposit Insurance Corporation (FDIC), through bans on "red lines" and credit disciplines. Capping it all off is tax deductibility for mortgage interest and $500,000 family home exemptions from capital gains taxes.

The self-referential loops of limitless money creation are the fundamental problem. Without reconnecting money to the reality of scarce time, no regulatory regime is going to work.

If the ultimate source of the value of money is the scarcity of time, what happens when central banks and governments eclipse the cost of time by spurning every settled measure for money—from gold to interest income? It seems that money migrates to the residual scarcity beyond time, land. The cost of space—represented by select urban real estate and agricultural land and the commodities that they support—goes through the roof.

Since even central banks cannot rescind the law of gravity, what goes through the roof ultimately returns to the ground. This is the well-known cycle of real estate boom and bust, exacerbated in recent years by compulsive securitization of mortgages. With unmoored money, unlinked to time, markets follow what engineers call a "hunting oscillation," gyrating spastically.

From Japan to Iceland, from Florida to Spain, a world of unmetered money has seen a twenty-first-century retreat from productive investment and a plunge into real estate and its finance. When money has no reliable metric but what it can buy, it migrates toward the visible and the palpable—an economy of now. A focus on existing assets leads to a shrinkage of investment horizons, a doldrums of growth, and an overhang of debt, marked by growing inequality and declining productivity.

The securitization of real estate does not even lead to more and better housing in response to market demands for shelter. A financial learning curve does not produce a learning curve in the construction of cheap housing. Driving information out of actual housing markets, financialization produces large discrepancies between the pattern of shelter supplies and actual needs and demands. In cities such as San Francisco and New York, which undergo so-called real estate booms, these discrepancies make housing scarcer and even increase homelessness.

Unmoored money unleashes financial hypertrophy, a tumescence of banking and other economic domains that feed on volatility and leverage. After 1970 the financial industry nearly tripled its share of the U.S. economy, and private credit nearly tripled its share of advanced-country GDP.

One group, however, is necessarily left behind. Incarcerated in time are nonfinancial wage and salary earners, paid by the hour or month. These time-bound employees are the foundation of much of the middle class and the real economy. Having tracked productivity gains in the years following World War II, workers' hourly wages plateaued after 1973, rising a total of only 8.9 percent in the years since, while productivity rose 243.6 percent. Harvesting most of the difference were the forces that could siphon the immeasurable sums of government money, capturing transfer payments and subsidies, banking and central banking loops and leverage, corporate mergers and buybacks, and real estate finance.

The information theory of money can explain the hypertrophy of finance, the migration of money to real estate, the gyration of markets, the imbalances of trade and capital movements, and the rise of inequality, all part of the continuing catalog of complaints of accountant-economists. Turner and Piketty are correct that banks have become parasitical shufflers of existing assets rather than productive investors in new projects. They are describing the shrinking of the horizons of investment and enterprise in an economy where money is freed from the constraints of time and entrepreneurs are shackled by governmental pettifoggery.

Bidding on existing assets, investors avoid the perils of creative long-term commitments. In a world where money has lost its meaning and investment is beclouded by capricious bureaucracy and government intervention, entrepreneurs seek ways to abate uncertainty. Rapid-fire investment and speculation take advantage of the volatility of all prices in the oceanic turbulence of currency trading. Flash boys develop strategies to deal with micro-regularities amid a random undulation rather than investing in long-term currents of creativity.

The Turner-Piketty thesis requires power to be centralized, money to be manipulated, and regulations to be expanded. But this approach is the root of the stagnation rather than the remedy for it.

What Turner and Piketty and their sponsor George Soros curiously fail to confront is the global ocean of currency trading, which is the alternative to money as a metric with secure roots in the constants of nature. These bold thinkers simply cannot conceive of real money as a measuring stick. They remain at sea, therefore, in a currency morass that all their policies would make still worse.

Chapter 10

Hypertrophy of Finance

With the fall of gold as a means of payment and as a unit of account (but not yet as a store of value)..., the world monetary system is not easy to understand. At least conceptually, the pre-1914 gold standard was simple: the domestic and international means of payment were the same.

—Ronald McKinnon (1979)[1]

What can an exchange rate really mean...when it changes by 30 percent or more in the space of 12 months only to reverse itself? What kind of signals does that send about where a businessman should intelligently invest? ... The answer to me must be that such large swings are a symptom of a system in disarray.

—Paul Volcker (1992)

I think [currency speculation] is better than currency restrictions, but a unified currency would be even better.

—George Soros (1995)

The idea of trekking back through twentieth-century history to excavate the ruins of the gold standard seems arrantly retrograde, like returning to quill pens, horse-drawn carriages, slavery, or wampum. After all, didn't John Maynard Keynes call gold a "barbarous relic"? To Paul Krugman, the gold standard is a "mystical" repetition of the "sin of Midas," worshipping a shiny metal. This is not a partisan issue. Krugman often cites Milton Friedman, who as early as 1951 made the case for banishing gold in favor of a free competitive float of currencies and fatefully counseled Richard Nixon to remove gold backing from the dollar in 1971.

Warren Buffett summed up the conventional view with his usual pith: "Gold gets dug out of the ground…we melt it down, dig another hole, bury it again and pay people to stand around guarding it…. Anyone from Mars would be scratching their head."[2]

The gold standard has moved beyond the pale of respectable thought. A bipartisan University of Chicago business school poll for a *Wall Street Journal* blog in 2012 found *zero support* for the gold standard. Forty-three percent of the surveyed economists "disagreed" with returning to gold, and an additional 57 percent "strongly disagreed."[3] That adds up to 100 percent, a "consensus" that might spark envy even in such hermetic circles of "settled science" as a UN séance on climate change.

With a limited total tonnage, which could be stored in a single small room, gold is seen to suffer from an acute deflationary bias. Since the basic money supply cannot expand significantly, it is believed that money prices, including wages and salaries, have to shrink.

Academics make the case that gold failed first under the stresses of World War I, when the combatant states defected, one after another, and most noncombatants followed. Then it failed again in the Depression of the 1930s, with recovery coming to countries in the exact order of their departure from gold. Finally it collapsed, seemingly for good, in the 1970s, when, with gold bleeding from the American trove of reserves and the French kibitzing sanctimoniously, Nixon tipped over the table and set up the dollar as the house money. His Texas swagman John Connally explained the sophisticated strategic calculation behind Nixon's move: "Foreigners are out to screw us. It's our job to screw them first." A system that is relinquished at every turn of the screw, gold seems a master too harsh and exacting for frail human capabilities.

Ultimately fatal for the gold standard were studies focused on the 1930s by some of the world's most respected economic statesmen and scholars. From Friedman and Krugman to former Fed chairman Ben Bernanke and former White House chief economic advisor Christina Romer (chosen by Obama for her mastery of depression economics), all ascribed the Great Depression chiefly to the monetary shackles of the gold standard. Friedman, who advised Richard Nixon on gold, did the most damage. In his magisterial *Monetary History of the United States, 1867–1960*, written with Anna Jacobson Schwartz,[4] he tied the Depression directly to the Fed's gold-based monetary policy that supposedly forced a 40 percent money supply collapse amid the carnage of failing banks between 1929 and 1931.

Crediting Friedman, Bernanke's influential paper "The Gold Standard, Deflation, and Financial Crisis in the Great Depression: An International Comparison"[5] focused on how the Depression ended. He showed that Japan bolted from the standard first in 1931, with Britain close behind, and that they led the world in recovery, followed by Germany (1932), the United States (1933), and recalcitrant, gold-grasping France (1936). After Roosevelt abandoned gold in 1933, as Romer points out, U.S. industrial output lurched up 57 percent between March and July, apparently exulting over escape from its gilded cage. It is clear that if you are in a global depression, with a third of the workforce unemployed and communists marching in the streets (and in the White House advising you on money), the best course may not be to sit around counting your ingots and reflecting on the gold backing of the Industrial Revolution.

A better, faster, truer replacement for the gold standard, we are to believe, is the high-technology "information standard." If you have an information economy with wealth as knowledge and growth as learning, you want a monetary system that rapidly conveys crucial information on prices in time and space. There has never been an information system so global, so fast, so robust, as the foreign exchange trading system of convertible currencies.

The late eminent banker Walter Wriston decades ago likened "the international financial markets…to a vote on the soundness of each country's fiscal and monetary policies…held in the trading rooms of the world every minute of every day…. This continuing direct plebiscite on the value of currencies and commodities proceeds by methods that are growing [ever] more sophisticated…."[6] The chief difference today is that the telephones and telex machines of the past have given way to half a trillion dollars' worth of supercomputer gear linked by fiber optic lines at the speed of light. The system now collects its information sixty million times faster, with hugely greater granularity, not by the minute but by the microsecond.

What's not to like? As Wriston noted in *The Twilight of Sovereignty* (1992), "Politicians...are right to complain. Not only are governments losing control over money, but this newly free money...is asserting its control over them...."[7] President Clinton's advisor James Carville famously expressed his wish "to be reincarnated as the bond market. It can intimidate anyone." Underlying the bond market is the currency market that determines bond values in every country. As Wriston asserted, "The old discipline of the gold standard has been replaced...by the new discipline of the Information Standard, more swift and draconian than the old."

As the venerable banker sternly admonished, quoting journalist Michael O'Neill, "There are no U-turns on the road to the future." This new information standard is irreversible, as fully established and demonstrably effective as any institution in the world economy. Implementing the new standard is the largest and most flexible, liquid, widely dispersed, and competitive— indeed, as economists claim, most "perfect"—market in the history of the planet.

Three-quarters of the business is in spot trades and simultaneous foreign exchange swaps in which one currency is traded for another, spot and forward simultaneously. By transacting both now and in the future at the same time, all exchange-rate risk is removed. Whether the rate changes or not, the bank is compensated for the exchanges. Designed to insulate currencies from market turbulence, these ploys also enable profitable arbitrage. In drastically smaller but still huge volumes—trillions a week— there are also outright forward currency buys and sells, derivative currency swaps, and forex options, as financiers employ ever more ingenious techniques to take advantage of volatile price changes.

This awesome multidimensional system, spanning the globe and extending into the future, enables any company anywhere at any moment, without risk, to exchange goods and services for money with customers in other countries. It enables world trade, globalization, integrated markets, and multinational corporations. It provides a cosmopolitan carpet for comity and commerce in the modern world. It garners profits and fees and margins for its providers and enables commerce for the companies that use the services.

This trading system for floating currencies is Milton Friedman's dream. But it also reflects the concept of "spontaneous order," a mainstay of the Austrian school of Friedrich Hayek and Ludwig von Mises. On the world's most advanced computer networks, it links the thousands of foreign exchange desks of all the major banks and other financial institutions, thousands of hedge funds and specialized dealers, and scores of principal trading funds (PTFs, mostly automated high-frequency operators, the so-called "flash boys"). It brings in multinational corporations that command sufficient international business to support their own trading desks. They all work in parallel, with no central coordination, to arrive instantaneously at convertible currency prices around the world.

Looming over the entire world economy, this web of exchange is also a part of the fabric of wealth creation and distribution, justice and growth. Just as land-based human beings tend to ignore the much larger portion of the earth's surface covered by the oceans, so individual consumers tend to focus on the energy, agricultural, manufacturing, and service businesses with which

they interact in their day-to-day lives and ignore the oceanic trading that surrounds and sustains them. But the volume of currency
exchange dwarfs by orders of magnitude all other economic
measurements—GDP, global trade, Internet transactions, industrial production, Google searches, global stock market exchanges,
global commodity values, and even derivatives.

Every three years, the Bank for International Settlements (BIS)
in Basel, Switzerland, adds it all up on a "net-net" basis adjusted
to nullify double counting from local and cross-border transfers
between dealers. By this careful metric, BIS in April 2013 identified
a flow of some *$5.3 trillion a day*, more than a third of all U.S.
annual GDP every twenty-four hours. The 2013 total signified
currency transactions throughout the year and around the globe
at a rate of more than $600 million every second.[8]

So how is it going? Measured by the rise in volumes cited by
BIS in 2013, it was a runaway success. Since the crash of 2001,
currency trading was up nearly fivefold. Since 2004, it was up
two and a half times. Since the crisis year of 2007, it had risen
160 percent. It is still apparently rising fast. BIS will give us the
details in 2016. Are you ready for an average billion-dollar trading second?

Providing entrepreneurs with accurate measurements of the
relative value of all the world's hundreds of different moneys, the
float makes fungible funds available on the spot without currency
risk. In other words, with vastly greater speed and automated
efficiency, the system performs the role previously played by the
gold standard, while at the same time enabling every country to
follow its own monetary policy. In light of this indispensable
double service, combining two apparently incompatible goals, no
one has complained about inadequate liquidity or performance.

Supremely banking intensive, the system channels all the world's commerce through the portals of the great international banks (just ten in the United States and fifteen in the United Kingdom) and enables them to collect fees. With 16.11 percent of the total trading in May 2015, the largest player is Citibank. Deutsche Bank ranks second with 14.54 percent. Outside the ten top banks, a small portion of the trading in the United States is dispersed among twenty-four other entities. For all the software apps for amateur currency trading, peer-to-peer freelancing is a drop in the ocean.

Participating in international commerce, every company must pay a toll to elite international banking intermediaries. The bankers love it. Trading and hedging currencies has become the chief generator of transactions volume at the giant banks and an important but far smaller source of profits (just ten banks totaled $21 billion in currency trading profits in 2008, while the world economy tanked). Much of the speculation cancels out in the wash. But currency trading is also an outreach leader for banks, engaging their international operations with all the leading multinationals.

By various measures, 90 to 97 percent of all the transactions are judged to be "speculative," devoted not to enabling trade in goods and services but to harvest profits and fees from arbitrage and leverage. Contrary to some claims, however, hedge funds are not the culprits. Only around one-tenth of the traffic in 2013 was ascribed by BIS to hedge funds and PTFs. Transacting some 77 percent of the business are ten leviathan banks in Western countries. These tolls and fees are burdens on global trade and economic growth paid by the production sector of the economy to the financial sector. But it is the sum of all these activities—hedging, speculation, and derivatives—that accounts for the oceanic span of liquid and available currency services.

As Friedman taught us, currency speculation can assure price stability. Speculation, in his view, could be destabilizing only if the speculators lost money. But money losers would eventually exit the market, leaving the profitable speculators (like those ten big U.S. banks full of computers and specialists) in charge, accurately arbitraging among the currencies and smoothing out the divergences. Thus, according to the experts, a massively speculative, oceanic market like currency trading, approaching the ideal of perfect competition, tends to an equilibrium of stable and accurate relative prices. To its exponents, this market's rapid growth attests to its usefulness and robust results.

Nonetheless, as one might suspect in the wake of the global crash led by the same big banks, the system is less than impeccable. The boom in currency traffic since 2001, 2004, and 2007 might imply that international trade was also booming. Trade in goods and services has indeed risen a total of 36 percent since the low in 2007, but currency trading has risen more than four times faster—160 percent. After 2011, trade flattened out while currency trading continued to rise, up 32 percent since 2010. No unexpected swell of trade explains the expansion of currency exchanges.

Dominating the system utterly is the West. In the forefront of the foreign exchange operations are the United States and Europe, with London's "City" alone accounting for 36 percent of all trading. Some 87 percent of transactions involve the dollar, in which 63 percent of all international trade is denominated and which accounts for more than half of all global reserves held by central banks to back their currencies. Since the economies of these leading traders in the West have failed to grow substantially, recovering from the slump but not moving on to significant new highs by 2016, currency trading and its effects constitute a substantial share of total growth.

That is what we mean by the "hypertrophy of finance," which accounts for 35 to 40 percent of corporate profits. While trade in goods and services languishes, currency trading soars. Financial service finds its ultimate test in how it affects the rest of the economy. But currency trading has been rising at least twenty times faster than productivity growth.

Does the West benefit from all this churn? Trade has grown most robustly in Asia and the emerging nations, led by China and its satellites and India. Yet China, Hong Kong, Singapore, and Taiwan—the spearhead of global trade expansion in recent decades—have all largely opted out of the floating-currency system. Against agonized protests from the West, they fix their currencies on the dollar as much as possible, and some of them impose controls on capital movements. Outside of the Asian emerging sector, world trade has inched up only slowly. Likewise world GDP growth.

As Wriston was the first to point out, this system provides a global "information standard" for currencies. If it takes between 35 and 40 percent of the profits of the economy to supply the information and to build the knowledge behind our twenty-first-century wealth, perhaps that is the price of progress in the information age. But as many have noticed, problems persist. A likely effect is inequality. If a large and probably increasing portion of all the profits in Western economies is skewed to a tiny elite of governmentally favored financiers in ten big banks, less income, presumably, flows to enterprise.

Currency trading is a hypertrophic manifestation of the "financialization" of the U.S. economy. Finance over the last decade has become an entente between government and banks, focused on precisely the least successful U.S. sectors. As Eric Janszen has pointed out: "[T]he incursion of finance into every aspect of American business and economic life...changed the way consumers buy automobiles and U.S. automakers run their businesses, the way students pay for school and universities fund their operations, the way homes are financed and consumer goods acquired. In short, credit became the biggest American business of all.... The entire economic system has been glued together by one profound fantasy: Finance can substitute for production and credit for real savings.... [But] governments cannot print either wealth or purchasing power. These must be earned."[9]

Wriston acknowledged that the result of this global plebiscite on moneys is an estimate of the *relative* values of the currencies in the float. In other words, in this microsecond engine of information, there is no anchor, no peg, no grid, no standard, no metric, no parity value. In mathematical theory, as Kurt Gödel proved, an information system must have axiomatic roots outside itself. As we have seen, self-referential and circular, a monetary system in all its global glory can roll off the edge of the world. In foreign exchange currency trading, values at times can become whatever the most powerful traders want them to be.

Without roots in outside reality, any system can be pushed off course by self-interested parties. If currencies are valued only in other currencies, there is no way to certify that the entire system is functioning in a beneficial way. The worldwide economic doldrums suggest that it isn't. There is little reason to expect self-referential global currency markets to gravitate toward a correct valuation of anything.

Yet the purpose of currencies is to enable real and reliable outcomes that correspond to economic truth and justice: optimal economic results and distributions. If financial profits are not in return for services that enrich the entire system, they are unjust. Bankers in one country should not be able to extort rents from microchip manufacturers in another country or from workers in another industry unless the banks are contributing real knowledge and learning.

One test of the currency trading system is its volatility. Do currencies gyrate more or less than the businesses and products, commodities and economies, payments and investments that they supposedly measure? The answer is obvious. Currencies go up and down far more frequently and violently than the economies behind them. Since 1990, for example, the economies of Japan and the United States have slowly diverged, U.S. GDP continuing to grow and Japan's remaining sluggish. Japanese monetary policy has in general been far looser than America's, but inflation has been flat. Interest rates in both countries were low to zero. On the surface, this scene would not seem to present promising opportunities for arbitrage.

Yet the yen-dollar rate has been all over the lot—far more volatile than the divergences in growth of the Japanese and U.S. economies. While currency traders exchanged hundreds of trillions of yen a day, the currency bounced around like a jitterbug. In currency trading, the movements are inverse: when the dollar rises in yen, the yen is falling in value. In 1990 the yen sank from 140 to the dollar to 160 and then leapt up to 120. The next year it tumbled down to 140 again, then in a series of jumps and gyrations it soared to 80 in 1995. By 1998 it had declined to 150, but it lurched back near 100 during the early 2000s, with plenty of bumps along the way. By 2002 it popped down to 135, and in 2004, with many passing adventures, it was a little above 100. And so on, appreciating ultimately in 2012 back to 80 yen to the dollar. Three years later it was back to 100.

This feckless juggling of measuring sticks provided endless opportunities for trading in securities denominated in the two currencies. Financial publications were full of descriptions of a lucrative "carry trade" by which bankers profited from irrational currency shifts and their effect on relative interest rates and bond prices.

As we have seen, a measuring stick more variable than what it measures does not promote equilibrium or stability. It exacerbates imbalances in the distribution of income and wealth, between financial and commercial corporations, and between politically favored and disadvantaged groups.

The international currency trading system is the alternative to gold. The world knows of the alleged flaws of gold. The flaws of the float are fundamental. A measuring stick cannot be part of what it measures. Currency trading is deeply embroiled in the world economy and its price system. A metric cannot be more volatile than what it measures. Currencies are drastically more volatile than the economic activity that they gauge. Thus floating currencies defeat the very function of money as a metric.

Controlled by governments, the float pushes politicians toward centralized solutions. An express purpose of floating currencies is to enable politicians to pursue insular economic policies. All too often these policies come at the expense of their citizens and of world economic growth.

Currency trading is vastly more voluminous than the traffic in goods and services that it enables. Its microsecond transactions are froth on the world economy with little or no informational significance. But with leverage, they can yield huge profits with no real economic productivity.

Currency trading is a playpen for financial predators. Because the holdings controlled by particular financiers and banks are so much larger than the economies of even sizable countries, intruders can upset the finances of countries with "hot money," make a fortune, and leave. George Soros, the patron of both Piketty and Turner, is the leading case in point, building his fortune with disruptive excursions into the currencies of Great Britain, Indonesia, and Thailand.

Currency trading concentrates income and wealth in the government-linked financial sectors of Western economies, bringing about maldistribution that arouses envy and resentment and demoralizes capitalism.

Currency prices cannot be shown to reflect any rational basis of valuation. Calculations of purchasing power parity (comparing buying power for particular goods in different countries) do not apply: the need for constant PPP computations shows the errancy of currency values. Different growth rates seem irrelevant: China has been growing fast for two decades with scarce impact on its currency. Interest rates seem deceptive: zero-rates are suspiciously associated with currency appreciation. Monetary policies seem feckless as countries around the world try, with majestic futility, to control their currencies.

The most reliable technique seems to be to target gold. That is what Paul Volcker did in 1984 in taming U.S. inflation. It is what Hjalmar Schacht did in 1924 to master the Weimarian inflation, releasing a new gold-based Rentenmark to replace the worthless Reichsmark. It is what the Brazilians did in 2002 finally to get newly real.

Perhaps the world economy should get real. It should contemplate a new tie to gold.

Chapter 11

Main Street
Pushed Aside

In the late autumn of 2015, a time of Trumpery and fantasy football, in the media and on the Internet, from all sides lamentations were heard for the plight of the American middle class.

The nation was in an economic slough. Defying five years of nominal "recovery," GDP numbers still slumped. Productivity growth, the source of new income, was stalled at 0.5 percent, 75 percent below the post–World War II average.[1] Interest rates—the money value of time—zeroed out the future and flattened savings, the source of all real investment, which remained sluggish. As job force participation rates sank back near 60 percent, real median annual household incomes continued their six-year slide, going from close to $60,000 in 2007 to $54,000 in 2014, well below their peak in 1989.

Economic pundits sought solace in the magic of monetary policy. Perhaps the Fed would raise interest rates, giving banks incentives to lend. Or perhaps it would continue its zero-interest-rate policy, maintaining business and household incentives to borrow. Or through some combination of quantitative easing with suitable "twists," might it do both at once?

Experts from Larry Summers to Ben Bernanke cite the failure of previous remedies as the reason to continue them. If zero interest rates have not ignited a recovery yet, perhaps their continuation can prevent a new recession. Perhaps negative interest rates could be contrived, requiring holders of cash to buy stamps every month to attach to their dollars. If five years of quantitative easing—some $4.6 trillion worth of bond purchases—could not reverse the five-year decline in real median incomes, perhaps another year would yield a trickle-down effect. The middle class might finally benefit. Or perhaps adding to the Fed's $1.7 trillion portfolio of mortgage-backed securities could rev up middle-class housing values.[2] It sure worked last time.

The entire system is backing, blindly and unguided, into the future. While professors and politicians inveigh against the depredations of the "rich," the rich, carefully disguised in bleached denim, slink away to their tax shelters. While the media are obsessed with immigration, immigrants decide to return home. And while Americans supposedly fret over the threat of foreign trade, the world suffers a rare seven-year 60 percent drop in the rate of trade growth in the midst of an alleged recovery.

The class-fraught rhetoric of both parties confirms an economy split along class lines, yet no class can prosper alone for long. We are all in this together, in a crucible of change up and down. A zero-sum game, in which any advance for some comes at the expense of others, zeroes out future growth for all. Middle-class prosperity consists not only in a sense of accomplishment and security but also in ownership and progress, in a productive triad of Main Street with Wall Street and Silicon Valley.

With the rise of the welfare state and the surge of payroll and healthcare taxes, wealth cannot consist of wages alone. Wages cannot sustain "middle-class" lifestyles, with traditional hopes for children and pensions for retirement. If the middle class isn't sharing in the growing equity of American business, supported through local banks and Wall Street, wages can be a wall of worry and insecurity, one step away from joblessness and penury.

But Wall Street cannot long thrive while bureaucrats wage war upon its freedoms, repress its creativity in webs of rules, and tame it with upside caps and downside guarantees. Silicon Valley's creativity needs a path through Wall Street and Main Street to an ascendant middle class and a peaceful and prosperous world.

During the boom years 1983–2000 under Reagan and Clinton, Main Street, Wall Street, and Silicon Valley meshed. Main Street prospered with the creation of millions of new businesses and some forty million net new jobs. Jobholders participated through their pensions in a Wall Street bonanza that ended with individual investors holding more than half the public shares of U.S. business. Spearheading the Wall Street expansion and the jobs boom were thousands of initial public offerings, from Apple and Genentech to Netscape and Qualcomm, the most lucrative coming from a carnival of invention in Silicon Valley.[3] American creativity ramified through a globalizing world economy, with the number of poor people living at the subsistence level of less than a dollar a day, adjusted for inflation, dropping by 20 percent. Markets battened on two billion new entrants into the middle classes from China and other emerging nations.

All seemed to be well with the monetary regime, dubbed the "great moderation" by Alan Greenspan, the guru of growth. But beneath a placid surface, the worldwide monetary system was breaking down.

Toward the end of the millennium, the world plunged into an Asian monetary debacle, the dot-com crash, the telecom debauch, and the Russian ruble meltdown. A thousand telecom companies went bankrupt. Many causes are cited—prodigal Asian capitalists, criminal telecom accountants and CEOs, dot-com-bubble hysteria, sinking oil prices, and Russian corruption, but the real source was monetary volatility.

An unexpected deflation of the dollar—appreciating by some 30 to 40 percent between 1996 and 1999 against most currencies and by 57 percent against gold—brought down all heavily indebted companies and dollar-denominated commodities. Oil, for example, dropped 44 percent between January 1996 and December 1998, from $17.94 to $9.80, which means that the oil price of dollars rose 83 percent. Meanwhile, the dollar measured in gold rose 138 grams, from 241 grams at its low in 1996 to 379 grams at its high in 1999.

Just as inflation bails out debtors and rewards creditors, unexpected deflation punishes debtors, who have to pay back their loans with more-valuable dollars. All prices became questionable. As the dollar soared, the neural webs of a globalizing economy— its price system and trading rules—broke down into "hot money" cascades and central bank freeze-ups. The prime victims were the Asian crisis economies, which borrowed heavily to defend their currencies against "hot money," and the global telecoms, which incurred huge debt to build worldwide fiber optic networks. Mandating fiber was the increasing video traffic of the ascendant Internet and its dot-com extravaganza.

The crash of 2000 downsized Silicon Valley and caused a collapse of small-business creation. But Main Street conjured with Wall Street to summon a new boom for the new century. Fueled by a stream of exotic securities backstopped by the federally supported insurers Fannie Mae and Freddie Mac, people began speculating on their own houses. Compensating for wage stagnation during this period was a national crescendo in real estate "equity," rising in "real terms" by 40 percent between 2001 and 2006. Copycat globalization spread the syndrome from Florida to Spain and Iceland.

This "real" housing appreciation was another monetary illusion. Housing is a consumption good; its appreciation always depends on the rising value of production and entrepreneurship surrounding it. Government subsidies, guarantees, and mortgage banking games aim to use federal power to convert a consumption binge into a savings and investment boom. But investment means a yield in the future, paying off the debts, expanding the equity. Housing appreciation from subsidized credit and reduced down payments does not sustain future payment streams.

Under capitalism, credit expansion is no substitute for real savings. To *save* is not a mere accounting trick. It means to forgo consumption, put off spending, and invest time in productive learning. It is a process of accumulating the knowledge to create new value for the future. It means not merely bidding up the worth of existing buildings, but building up real wealth through tested new business knowledge.

Under capitalism, the middle-class Main Street passes through a global web of interconnections. The web of middle-class net worth embraces Wall Street and Silicon Valley, energy enterprise and medical progress, first-world innovation and third-world development, Brazilian coffee plantations and Korean electronics, Chinese manufacturing and Israeli invention. The Main Street middle rises through a combination of earnings, education, and capital gains around the world.

It begins with start-ups. Some 64 percent of the new U.S. jobs created between 2002 and 2010 came from twenty-three million small businesses with fewer than five hundred employees, companies that are the foundation of middle-class prosperity. In each of the four most recent U.S. recoveries, the small-business sector spearheaded the revival, growing sharply faster than the Fortune 500. In the lapsed lift-off since 2009, though, jobs at small firms have actually declined. Only large firms expanded employment.

The jobs that sustain middle-class prosperity feed on expanded enterprise and investment, equity and innovation. In the United States, some two-thirds of all stock market appreciation over the last thirty-five years came from companies supported by venture capital—what we call "Silicon Valley" for short, which now reaches from Palo Alto to Austin and even Tel Aviv. Most of the rest of our wealth creation reflects the process of globalization, as emerging economies like China and India duplicate the economic development of Europe and North America. Consolidating the gains are U.S. and European "platform companies" designing products to be manufactured in Asia and marketed around the world, with Western companies historically harvesting most of the profits.[4]

Without the synergistic triad of invention, investment, and distribution—Silicon Valley, Wall Street, and Main Street—the middle class decays. Policy-makers are right to focus on middle-class prosperity as long as they remember that middle-class growth depends on invention and high-tech immigration.

Silicon Valley in 2016 seems buoyant. In 2014 venture capital investment reached $48 billion, and in 2015 it rose still higher, to a level unseen since the 2000 peak. But the recent rise reflects the depth of the slump. The 2014 total is merely one-third of the $144 billion (in 2015 dollars) raised for twice as many companies in 2000.

More important is the allocation of 2015 venture funds. Seed-stage investments in start-ups dropped to their lowest level since 2002. There were fewer than half as many IPOs as in 2000, and they were focused on a few large deals. Meanwhile, in Silicon Valley, venturers ruminate on an incursion of "unicorns"—some 130 private companies now with official valuations close to a billion dollars apiece, for a total market cap approaching half a trillion dollars.

In the ordinary history of Silicon Valley, no private company but Apple obtained anything close to a billion-dollar market cap. Intel, Microsoft, Oracle, Cisco, and other Silicon Valley stars only reached that level through IPOs that led into long years of appreciation of their stocks as public companies. Most companies, including the most lucrative high-tech names—firms like Linear Technology and Applied Materials, Oracle and Sun Microsystems, Cisco, Amazon, and Qualcomm—were happy to go public at a market cap of a few score million. Even Microsoft did not reach near a market cap of a billion dollars until its IPO. Apple, which turned out to be the best stock of the last hundred years, went public at a valuation of $1.3 billion and eventually was valued by Wall Street at more than five hundred times that amount. Adjusted for inflation, Microsoft gained a comparable multiple in the public markets.

The bulk of the appreciation from these Silicon Valley IPOs thus went to Main Street, which held its shares through Wall Street in the form of pensions and stock holdings. Venture capitalists did well, but the broad middle class captured a large share of the returns.

By comparison, Facebook had an $80 billion IPO, from which the U.S. Securities and Exchange Commission "protected" the middle class by barring all but "qualified investors" from pre-IPO markets. The thousandfold gains from Facebook were reserved for the officially certified rich, the fortunate few venture capitalists and investors "qualified" as sufficiently well-off to make such a "risky" investment.

In the past, getting that gigabuck valuation required putting on a "road show" in which executives conjured up the company's roseate future for major public investment companies that acted in behalf of middle-class stockholders. This start-up process of "going public" prepared an initial public offering for masses of investors around the globe. It has been the spearhead of U.S. economic growth.

Today's "unicorn" valuations totaling hundreds of billions of dollars all took place without "going public." Pre-public investors anticipate something like a sevenfold return in exchange for the risk and illiquidity of pre-IPO markets. Thus the unicorn valuations imply projected exits—"liquidity events" and greater-fool financings—seven times higher. If the public could be induced to buy these companies after the initial surge of their market cap, the anticipated harvest over the next few years would be a couple trillion dollars, most of it going to "qualified investors," that is, the "rich." The middle class would be holding the bag.

On the surface, the emergence of hundreds of companies with billion-dollar valuations is supremely promising. From Intel to Facebook, similar venture-based companies in the past have accounted for some 21 percent of our GDP and 60 percent of stock market capitalization. Venture companies are the prime source of American growth. But this time seems to be different. The chief concern is whether these "unicorns" portend a "new bubble." Would these virtual worlds and software virtuosos pop and piffle like 1999's dot-com web-vanities and Petco litter boxes?

"Software," as the preeminent venturer Marc Andreessen says, "eats up the world." Uber may transform urban transport, Pinterest may reinvent online advertising, Palantir may offer a radical advance in big data for security and even boast a billion in revenue and a role in finding Osama bin Laden. But folks may finally "swipe left" by Tinder and the scores of other multibillion bit-monkey mock-ups. The world may prove treacherous even for instant virtual hooker drone delivery systems.

Back in 1999, the exits opened out into capacious public markets through IPOs, then seven times more numerous than mergers and acquisitions (M&As) for tech companies. But today the rarities are IPOs, outnumbered by M&As twenty-two to one. Which means that the "greater fools" chiefly targeted by venture capitalists to buy their unicorns are not you and I and millions of others in a possibly hallucinogenic NASDAQ public market but rather a tiny elite of cagey bidders counseled by game theory quants. The oligopsonists include Facebook's Mark Zuckerberg,

Microsoft's Satya Nadella, Google's alphabetic Larry Page, Disney's Robert Iger, Verizon's Lowell McAdam, Amazon's Jeff Bezos, Netflix's Reed Hastings, and Apple's Tim Cook. None seems a good bet for a gaggle of gulls.

What is really going on is the displacement of the open and rabble-run IPO market by an exclusive game of horse trading among the most exalted elite of "qualified investors," the owners of the leviathans of the last generation of IPOs. Capped by such regulatory tolls and encumbrances as the accounting mazes of Sarbanes-Oxley, Fair Disclosure's code of omertà, and the EPA's "cautionary principle" barring innovative manufacturing, the new Silicon Valley confines ascendant companies beneath a glass ceiling. From Apple to Google, a few public giants dominate this private-company market since they are the only potential buyers. Within this confined space, every titan is more eager to purchase his start-up rivals than to compete with them.

Whitewashed and fitted out with shiny horns, the aspiring "unicorns" shuffle through the corrals of Sand Hill Road and the carrels of Cupertino, seeking sustenance from smart-set venture capitalists and international tech tycoons. With their high-calorie burn rates and weak revenues, these creatures survive on a continued boom in reveries.

The tycoons swipe left or swap right, sending the nags off to the races or back to the stables—or perhaps the glue factory. Whether this one-horn hippodrome of venture capital constitutes an expanding "bubble" or a balky bottleneck, it is a bad circulatory system for finance: a traffic jam on Route 101 with no easy exit to Wall Street.

Yet the *New York Times* and *Vanity Fair* tech scribe Nick Bilton reports that there is a redeemer on the horizon, filling the tech financiers and their clients with high hopes. It's the Federal Reserve Bank: "The Fed's decision to carry out multiple rounds of quantitative easing, in which the central bank stimulates the economy by buying securities, has flooded the system with cash."[5]

So there we have it. The unicorn buyer of last resort will be the Fed. The "lender of last resort" for the financial system, the governmental guarantor for all the big banks and other "systemically important financial institutions," the backup reinsurer for windmill Quixotes, ethanol pushers, and solar prospectors, the last ditch for Fannie Mae and Freddie Mac and other mortgage packagers, the default financier for the trillions of dollars of student loans, for veterans' hospitals, for underfunded pensions and Medicaid reserves of the states, and above all for the proliferating securities and insecurities of the federal government, this same federal fount of funds and faith is also seen as the savior of Silicon Valley. What assures a soft landing for the hang-gliding unicorns is the Fed. Is the ultimate symbol of our predicament not a bailout for middle-class mortgages but a backup of imaginary money for mythical beasts?

In the new world of zero interest rates and quantitative ease, money migrates not to opportunity but to bureaucracy, not to creativity but to clout and cozenage, not to new 3-D semiconductors but to sleek Solyndras. Without real interest rates, funds flow to influence and precedence. Confined below the Fed's ceiling, venture capitalists are left to play circle games with unicorns.

Only large companies can master the demands of the game, the need for foreign exchange hedges, transnational holding companies, legal specialists, complex securitizations, intellectual property swaps, private equity inversions, multiple stock classes, alternative energy entanglements, audit committees, double cross-checking accountant teams, diversity mandates, sexual harassment backside protectors, and other pettifoggery all crowding out the entrepreneurs.

The test of an entrepreneurial idea is its experimental and empirical truth, affirmed by profitability. In a knowledge economy, cash is valuable only if it is validated by real learning. That is the moral foundation of capitalist wealth and the only source of growth.

"Flooding the system with cash" is bad for the economy because it falsifies price signals and demoralizes capitalists by misrepresenting the outcomes of entrepreneurial experiments. If capital is free, businesses substitute it for labor, which becomes relatively costly. Money shufflers triumph over job creators.[6] Growth slows, employment lags, and Silicon Valley becomes just another vector of the monetary state.

Worse, current monetary policy is fostering class war; it is profoundly unfair to ordinary workers as well as entrepreneurs. Zero interest rates rob future generations by bidding up the value of current government assets and privileges. A bubble of current assets inflated by near-zero-interest loans does nothing to fund the future. Retirees face a prospect of shriveled pensions and support and watching their children and grandchildren live slow-motion lives.

According to the Fed's own data, from 2010 to 2015 some 62 percent of Fed money creation was recycled through the banks to the Treasury trough.[7] More than 65 percent of the rest went to a few large corporations, which continued to use it to suck up their own shares at a rate of $25 billion per month.

Our Federal Reserve System, which gives twelve bankers a monopoly on money, is broken. Its fruits are low growth, a shrinking job force, inequality, inefficiency, and a hypertrophy of finance. Nonproductive elites capture the bulk of the returns from money manipulation under government guarantees, and the rest of the population lives on financial leftovers.

The Fed has become a fourth branch of government that alienates Main Street from Wall Street and Wall Street from Silicon Valley. Our society is breaking up into separate and suspicious tribes ruled by federal bureaucrats deciding what money is worth and who gets it.

Our aging Federal Reserve System starves both small businesses and Silicon Valley of the capital needed to grow jobs and wages. Fed policy translates into zero-interest-rate loans for the government and its cronies, and little or nothing for savers or small businesses. And it has transformed Wall Street from an engine of innovation into a servant of government power.

Chapter 12

Wall Street Sells Its Soul

The current world monetary and economic system favors this new Wall Street currency regime over both Main Street and Silicon Valley. Once associated with research, analysis, and support for the independent enterprises of America, the new Wall Street simply means giant banks informally nationalized by Washington.

Deutsche Bank, Goldman Sachs, Morgan Stanley, UBS, Citibank, JPMorgan Chase, and the rest, eminent institutions all, are full of dazzling financial prestidigitators. But they are too big to fail and too dependent on government to succeed. Their horizons are too short to foster entrepreneurial wealth and growth. The bulk of financial profits now comes from "proprietary trading," with a time horizon measured in minutes and weeks rather than years and decades. They impart liquidity but not learning.

They are profitable because of a vast transfer of wealth away from workers and savers to bankers.

These institutions insidiously thrive by serving government rather than entrepreneurs. Government policy now favors the short-term arbitrage and rapid trading of the big banks over the long-term commitments that foster employment and growth, leaving us with a predatory zero-sum economy that destroys the jobs and depletes the incomes of the middle class.

For most of us, wildly changing prices and currency values are a menace. They confuse enterprise and learning and thwart the enduring commitments and investments that shape our lives and prospects. But the new Wall Street—with its computer-driven trading—thrives on volatility, enjoying protection on the downside from the government. Gyrations in currency and stock values, whether up or down, mean opportunities for arbitrage and fast trading. The new Wall Street harvests these gains through cheap borrowing from the Fed and accelerated buying and shorting of currencies and securities. Main Street and Silicon Valley, on the other hand, want stable currencies for the benefit of work, savings, and long-term investment, with the upsides protected by the rule of law.

The new Wall Street mostly welcomes Luddite environmental regulations that thwart manufacturing and promote litigation. But regulatory overreach and litigation paralyze Main Street and all but the lawyered leviathans of Silicon Valley. Favoring financial power over entrepreneurial knowledge, government policies have crippled the American jobs machine that led the world in the 1980s and 1990s and sustained income growth for nearly all Americans.

The new Wall Street delights in the spiral of guaranteed loans to college students, which expand the ledgers of banks and the investible endowments of universities, while Main Street and Silicon Valley suffer from the debt-driven flight from marriage and entrepreneurship of entire generations of debt-burdened college graduates (or worse, nongraduates).[1]

When large companies buy up their own shares and the shares of their potential competitors, the price of the remaining shares may move up. But the benefit to elite company stock values comes at the cost of a stagnant economy, without new competition and learning, jobs and growth.

Part of the problem is what I call the "outsider trading scandal." Hounded by government insider-trading witch hunts and "fair disclosure laws," investors must follow the government rule of "Don't invest in anything you know about." The only thing governments want the public to invest in is the state lottery, "where no one knows more than you."

Outside traders use market statistics and quarterly earnings correlations to guide ever more evanescent transactions. Since entrepreneurial learning comes from deep inside companies and requires intimate special knowledge, a ban on trading by anyone with inside knowledge impels investors away from close company analysis and productive finance.

In the face of the protean rules of the Securities and Exchange Commission and computerized investigations, it is simply foolhardy for a bank or hedge fund to base its public investments on real, unique inside knowledge. Nearly anyone who understands a company is barred from investing in it. Members of a company's board of directors, for example, who can always be judged to possess some incriminating inside insight, are basically prohibited from buying shares in the companies they know best. They are safe only if they lose money. The SEC, astoundingly, favors boards that know nothing about the companies they rule and have no stake in them. Lawyers and accountants proliferate. The SEC thus stultifies investment by pushing it into the hands of arrogantly ignorant outside traders.

Even mutual funds and other stock market investors are increasingly shunning actual investigation of particular firms. Intimidated by regulators, many funds do virtually no analysis of companies beyond the computerized parsing of balance sheets and quarterly statements for data used in fast-trading algorithms.

Under this self-defeating regime, the returns have migrated to large conglomerateurs and private equity players who benefit from perfectly legal insider trading in every one of their investments. Cagey private equity investors now can make lucrative gains by taking small public companies private and removing all the costly government-imposed impediments of redundant legal compliance and accounting pettifoggery.

Warren Buffett's Berkshire Hathaway and Jeffrey Immelt's General Electric, to take two prominent examples, are not real corporations but legal inside traders that allocate investments among diverse company holdings that they understand intimately. Likewise, venture capitalists and private equity players never make an investment without intimate investigation of every inside nook and cranny.

Guided by deep inside knowledge, venture capital is the most valuable money in the economy. Launching learning curves across a wide span of innovations, venturers have seeded companies that now produce some 21 percent of America's GDP, 65 percent of its market capitalization, and a probably underestimated 17 percent of its jobs.[2]

But venture capital represents a tiny proportion—less than 0.2 percent—of total capital. Deploying most capital are global conglomerates like Berkshire Hathaway and General Electric. They are a net positive force in the economy, but most of them contribute comparatively little of the innovation that yields real economic growth, jobs, and learning.

With little access to the venture capital or private equity game, the public at large is counseled to invest its money in "index funds." These yield no more knowledge and learning than the state lotteries do. Purchasing a sampling of all the stocks in the market without any research on specific companies, indexers give the public some exposure to the gains of the inside-trading conglomerateurs. But they provide less than no benefit to the learning processes that create growth and wealth. Index funds are parasites on the research done by actual investors.

Index funds are even worse than they look because they base allocation not on the expected yield of the investment but on market capitalization. As companies grow overvalued, they become an ever-larger share of the holdings of the funds. The anomalous rise of Apple to the world's most valuable corporation has saved the careers of thousands of managers. Momentum prevails until it stops. But as the economist Charles Gave of Gavekal puts it, "In a true capitalist system, the rule is the higher the price the lower the demand. With indexation, the higher the price, the higher the demand. This is insane."[3]

Yet as pioneered by the laureled John Bogle at Vanguard and encouraged by the SEC's insider-trading phobias, these parasitical and distortionary index funds directly extinguish knowledge and learning in the economy.[4] Vanguard now passively "manages" some $2.9 *trillion* of assets while contributing nothing to the investment process. Rather than investing in the market, they parasitically infest and congest it. Rather than creating wealth and jobs, they destroy them.

Dwarfing all positive investment by "inside traders" and knowledge brokers are the financial power brokers in the major banks. Thriving through leverage and arbitrage, fast trading and risk shuffling, they have long had access to virtually unlimited funds at near-zero interest rates, while the government has anointed most of them as too big to fail. In effect, the federal government, through the Federal Reserve and scores of other regulators, has socialized the downside of these institutions, enabling them to carry on what they call "creative risk taking." But what in fact they do is cockeyed extension of ever more cantilevered loans and compound securities with only tiny slivers of actual equity at risk. Real entrepreneurial risk taking is totally unrelated to mere hypertrophy of leverage with implicit government guarantees.

During the doldrums decade of the dot-com crash and the great financial recession, 2000 to 2010, the socialized big banks feasted on zero-interest-rate money from the Fed, bought trillions of dollars' worth of government bonds, and harvested the spread. From the Fed, they received over a trillion dollars of surreptitious largesse.[5]

These gains for bankers and governments were defrayed by the taxpayers and shareholders and even retirees through the zero-interest-rate policy.[6] When something is free, only the well-connected get much of it. Main Street is far back in the queue. Zero interest rates resulted in easy money for highly leveraged Wall Street speculators, cheap money for the government, and a parched credit landscape for entrepreneurial small businesses.

Some 2,600 community banks went out of business, too small to bail.

Velocity is frequency in money—how many times a dollar turns over in a year. Money is a wave phenomenon. Since the power of a wave rises with the square of its amplitude, large and long investments would be exponentially more significant than a series of small trades. Wavelets would be exponentially less potent than tsunamis. Thousands of fast trades do not add up to a program of high-impact investment for the economy.

Small and temporary anomalies are unsurprising and low entropy. Profits that reflect mere leverage or borrowing power do not usually contribute to the learning process. They reveal willingness to accept a level of calculable risk rather than singularities of creative learning. Such profits are predictable and thus low entropy.

The Stanford physicist and Nobel laureate Robert Laughlin has derided the elaborate efforts of scientists to find significance in the intrinsically transitory forms that arise on their computers during phase changes, such as bubbles in water on the brink of a boil.[7] These computational figments have an analogue here in the outside traders' search for momentary correlations. As Claude Shannon knew, *in principle* a creative pattern of data points— reflecting long and purposeful preparation and invention—is indistinguishable from a random pattern. Both are high entropy. Parsing of random patterns for transitory correlations fails to yield new knowledge. You cannot meaningfully study the ups and downs of the market with an oscilloscope. You need a microscope, exploring inside the cells of individual companies.

Currency values should be stable. In information theory terms, they should function as low-entropy carriers for high-entropy creations. But the oceanic currency markets are full of Laughlin froth to be parsed by computers for short-term anomalies. With leverage, these trades may accumulate to massive profits. But these profits do not contribute much to the processes of entropic learning that constitute all economic growth in an economy of knowledge.

A monetary reform could free banks from their current trivialization as government tools and make them once again crucial vessels of investment. In any banking system, the reason the maturities do not match is the divergence between the motivations of savers and the sources of the value of savings. Savers attempt to preserve their wealth in a liquid form, where they can retrieve it whenever they wish. But the laws of irreversible time ordain that money cannot stand still or uncommitted without losing value.

For its perpetuation and expansion, the wealth in banks is utterly dependent on long-term investments in perilous processes of learning—real investments in companies and projects that can fail at any time. The role of banks is to transform the savers' quest for security and liquidity into the entrepreneurs' necessarily long-term illiquidity and acceptance of risk. Without banks performing this role, economic growth flags and stagnation prevails, as Lawrence Summers and Robert Gordon observe.[8]

Explaining the sources of Britain's dominance of world trade, the Victorian journalist Walter Bagehot pointed to the vastly larger agglomerations of capital in London banks:

> A million in the hands of a single banker is a great power; he can at once lend it where he will, and borrowers can come to him, because they know or believe that he has it. But the same sum scattered in tens and

fifties through a whole nation is no power at all: no one knows where to find it or whom to ask for it. Concentration of money in banks, though not the sole cause, is the primary cause which has made the money market of England so exceedingly rich, so much beyond that of other countries.[9]

Bagehot, the editor of the *Economist* from 1860 to 1877, saw the power of leverage as a force for economic diversity and dynamism, enabling small entrepreneurs to outperform established capital. He gives the example of a start-up using leverage to outperform an established company avoiding risk. Even while paying back its loan, or equity investment, the start-up can disrupt the established player by offering new and cheaper goods. "The egalitarianism of money," he wrote, "how it likes ideas better than it likes established capital, is very unpopular in many quarters."

"Banking is a profitable trade," he concluded, "because bankers are few and depositors myriad.... No similar system arose elsewhere, and in consequence London is full of money and all continental cities are empty as compared with it."

Bagehot compared banking with enterprise: "The banker must always be looking behind him seeing he has enough reserves. Adventure is the life of commerce, but caution—I had almost said timidity—is the life of banking. Merchants use their own capital rather than other people's money."

A key to the 2008 crash was some bankers' discovery of the temptations of other people's money when insured by government. Understanding this temptation, Bagehot warned against bailing out banks. "The cardinal maxim [of banking policy]," he wrote, "is that any aid to a present bad Bank is the surest mode of preventing the establishment of a future good Bank."

He commented on the inconsistency of central banking, even in that era, with a system of democratic government: "A bank of issue, which need not pay its notes in cash, has a charmed life; it can lend what it wishes, and issue what it likes, with no fear of harm to itself, and with no substantial check but its own inclination." Bagehot had many ideas for a better system. But his final observation remains hard to deny. "Dependence on the [central bank] is fixed in our national habits."

There is a difference, however. Bagehot was writing about a Newtonian world. The currencies central banks manage today have no anchor in gold and thus suffer from the same self-referential circularity that imperils all logical systems unmoored to outside foundations of reality. The U.S. Federal Reserve lives Bagehot's "charmed life": "It can lend what it wishes, and issue what it likes." Its unmoored money can be manipulated at will in the interests of its sponsors in government and their pseudo-private cronies, selling their souls to the Fed.

Chapter 13

A Wrinkle in Time

*Time is the coin of your life. It is the only coin you have,
and only you can determine how it will be spent. Be careful lest you let other people spend it for you.*

—Carl Sandburg

Money as time may be a lumpy lemma to swallow. Surely
money is many other things, from purchasing medium
to standard of value to store of worth. Money specifies
irreversible contracts and transactions, bonds and bids, and it
transmits signals of conditions far beyond its locality. A friend
once asserted to me that everything in the social sciences is either
wrong or self-evident. Is money as time an example of both?

Time may seem to be no more a facet of money than air or
water is. Is money as time merely a figure of speech or a glib
epigram?

I don't think so, because I don't think money is merely a func-
tional tool. Like Ayn Rand, who wanted a dollar sign embossed
on her coffin, I believe money possesses transcendent significance.
Because we use it to prioritize most of our activities, register and

endow our accomplishments of learning and invention, and organize the life-sustaining work of our society, money is more than a mere payments system. It expresses a system of the world. That is why I link it to the information theory of Kurt Gödel, Alan Turing, and Claude Shannon.

Each of these thinkers attempted to define his philosophy in utilitarian and determinist mathematics. Addressing pure logic as math, Gödel concluded that even arithmetic cannot constitute a complete and coherent system. All logical schemes have to move beyond self-referential circularity and invoke axioms outside themselves. Turing explored the possibility of a complete and self-sufficient logical machine and found it an impossible dream. His "Turing machine" defined the abstract logical architecture of all computers. But all computers must depend on what Turing called human "oracles" to define their symbols, instructions, and programs and to interpret their output, which as a stream of off-and-on currents or charges is ostensibly meaningless.[1] Shannon set out to create a purely mathematical definition of information and ended up providing a logical scheme of communication that depends on human subjectivity and creativity for meaning and purpose.

As a complex expression of logic and information, money represents an obvious frontier for information theory. As a logical scheme, it must have an axiomatic foundation beyond itself. It cannot endure as a trivial tautology in which its value stems from what it buys and is valued by it. That route always ends in a crash or inflationary binge, demanding the crisis-management tools of government institutions.

As a paramount expression of our computational and networked economy, money is an information system. Shannon's value-neutral definition of information as entropy or surprise liberated thousands of engineers to design computer and network systems—the cybernet fabric of our civilization. They did not concern themselves with the meaning, value, factuality, truth, consistency, or importance of the communication they enabled.

Today, however, the Internet is suffering the effects of these necessary limitations of engineering science. The net has to resort to trusted third parties outside the net to sustain its transactions. The resulting extra costs bar micropayments. Without an anchor in a system of reliable values, Internet offerings gyrate between free hustles and egregious gouges. The net also exhibits an inability to prioritize its activities, certify its claims, price its services, administer its ubiquitous "contracts," or notarize titles. The Internet offers crowning testimony both of Shannon's genius and the Gödelian incompleteness of his work.

Now, for the first time since the inception of our information society, we are moving toward what might be termed a new system of the world. At its heart is the development of a new monetary system based on a deeper reality than the minutes of the latest meeting of the eminent governors of the Federal Reserve Board. Bankers, politicians, academics, and bureaucrats alike must stop treating money as a manipulable tool of policy.

Essential to any system of the world, money extends its sway over monarchs and presidents, parliaments and prime ministers, generals and imams, despots and democrats. All must bow to a regime of laws and constraints that subordinate power to knowledge.

As Ludwig von Mises wrote, economics "did more to transform human thinking than any other scientific theory before or since," because "with good men and strong governments everything was considered feasible.... [But with the advent of economic science] now it was learned that in the social realm too there is something operative which power and force are unable to alter and to which they must adjust themselves if they hope to achieve success, in precisely the same way as they must take into account the laws of nature."[2] Among the ascendant laws of nature in the new system of the world are the findings of information theory.

These laws intersect with physical and chemical laws and must be compatible with them. But economic laws cannot be reduced to the material domain. Higher in the hierarchies of knowledge and learning than the rules of physical factors and forces,[3] money transcends determinism and enables creativity and freedom.

Austrian economists such as Mises have long held that all value is subjective. Their logic remains firm. As Gödel discovered and Shannon implied, even a measure of information depends on outside judgment and interpretation. This subjectivity of value, however, functions in a matrix of objective time. Time is the one economic factor that is irrefutably objective and thus lends objective substance to the subjectively driven movements of money.

Bounding every human activity is the inexorable influence of time. The winged chariot, the grim reaper, the forced march, the Heraclitean stream—all are common tropes in literature as in life. But money is about time in a more direct, far-reaching, integral, metrical, analytical, and dispositive way than any other human instrument.

The alternative to money is barter—direct exchanges of goods, without systems of storage and distribution. Imagine the valuation of bartered items in a primitive economy and you immediately confront the centrality of time. What determines how much of each item for trade is available is the time it takes to produce an incremental unit.

A house takes more time to make than a hammer. So, very roughly considered, a house might be worth many hammers. Intuitively, different time requirements make a horse more valuable than an apple, a pair of shoes more valuable than a coconut. As the common element in all goods and services, time determines the possibilities for exchange. As a barter economy becomes a commercial economy, these common time factors become manifested in money.

The tie between money and time is obvious in the case of loans and savings governed by the "time value of money," reflected by interest rates. These central capitalist functions still arouse anger and confusion. The French moralist Thomas Piketty sums them up as the exactions of "capital" and the bounties of the "rentier."[4] Dismissing the linkage of time and money as optional and even reprehensible, Piketty follows in the footsteps of philosophers and kings, priests and scholars who for millennia have ruminated restively on the morality and legitimacy of interest payments.

For centuries both the Catholic and the Islamic faiths condemned the exaction of interest as "usury." Moral human beings were not supposed to be realistic about the time domain of life. The future, present, and past converged in heaven, in a moral universe occupied by high-minded thinkers. Aristocrats everywhere learned to deprecate practical men wielding ledgers and calendars, clocks and actuarial tables. Hitler's case against the Jews fed on the idea that the yield of finance was somehow meretricious or extortionate, unnatural or treacherous.[5] The literary archetypes of lenders and savers are Shylock and Scrooge. A lender was supposed to deny that all that mattered in the transaction was the date of the loan and when he could retrieve the money and loan it out again. Recognizing that money translates to time would make interest payments as obviously legitimate as they are.

The inverse of interest on the bank's loans is interest paid on savings or deposits, which are loans by customers to a bank or other firm. According to the exponents of zero-interest-rate policy and to Piketty and to the other passionate advocates of reviving economies with inflation, these returns are also optional or arbitrary. Their arguments focus on the "maldistribution" of wealth or the unfairness of debt burdens, particularly when borne by democratic governments. By manipulating money as an instrument of policy, controlling the interest rates that they pay on their own debts, and fostering devaluation of their currencies, governments—and the economists who counsel them—are engaged in a futile and economically destructive war against time.

In physics, the source of the arrow of time is entropy. According to the second law of thermodynamics, the physical processes of the universe convert energy from usable forms into unusable forms, from potential energy at the top of the falls into kinetic energy flowing over the Hoover Dam, into less-available energy down the river to the sea.

Sadi Carnot defined entropy in the nineteenth-century context of steam engines.[6] He calculated the flow of heat from hot elements to cooler ones and the impossibility of reversing the process without supplying new energy from outside. Journalists routinely cite their breakfast eggs or the creamer diffusing through their coffee as examples of the irreversibility of entropic processes. Economists and ecologists cite entropy as the reason for the alleged exhaustion of natural resources or the inability of the planet to sustain continued growth of human populations.[7]

Ludwig Boltzmann was the first to link entropic processes to disorder and thus to information.[8] Claude Shannon was the first to link disorder to informative surprise and thus to creativity. Hubert Yockey showed that even in biology it is intrinsically impossible to distinguish a set of random data from the data points of a series of creative surprises.[9] Physics today breaks down into a school regarding the universe as randomness ordered only by an infinite multiverse and a school upholding a single universe ordered by creation and creativity.[10]

As shown by information theory, an entrepreneur launching an invention or new technology that unexpectedly changes our lives, a scholar demonstrating a new theory with a falsifiable proof, or a scientist identifying a new source of energy in defiance of expectations exhibits entropy just as surely and irreversibly as a glacier calving into the Arctic Ocean or an aged building shedding paint and shingles. Like thermodynamic entropy, information entropy conveys disorder, not order. Order and determinism represent the fulfillment of expectations; they are low entropy, while disorder and freedom are high entropy.

Information theory does not espouse chaos or anarchy. Shannon demonstrated that it takes a low-entropy carrier—a predictable channel with no surprises—to bear high-entropy messages full of surprising content. Because a random stream of bits is indistinguishable from a burst of unexpected and surprising creativity, Shannon showed, you do not want an entropic or surprising carrier or a noisy channel. The reason much of the world's information is migrating toward the electromagnetic spectrum is its low-entropy predictability guaranteed by the speed of light, the inexorable rule of time. Predictable electromagnetic carriers enable the receiver of messages to differentiate them from the carrier at the other end of the line.

The economics of information theory link money with time, the most fundamental and irreversible carrier in the universe. Money is not the content of transactions; it is the carrier. The use of money, however, enables the transmission of high-entropy information. The worldwide webs of glass and light and air that form the low-entropy channels of the Internet bear no more important, or high-entropy, "news" than the worldwide web of price signals.

Ernst Mach's "principle" in physics holds that unfathomable forces across the entire universe, summed at any particular point, shape the conditions at any given location on earth.[11] Mach's principle also applies to market economics, and even nonmarket economies cannot escape it. Every price is the expression of a worldwide fabric of other prices, conveyed by money, rooted in time. If the roots are torn up by governments—pulling up the carrots to check if they are ripe—the price system will convey false messages and stifle the learning and discovery that constitute all economic growth and progress.

Scientists have long appreciated the critical role of universal units of measurement in economics and industry. Builders of bridges and skyscrapers and electronic systems obtain components from around the globe. In order for these components to work with other components, their users must trust in immutable systems of measurement.

The International System of Units (known by the abbreviation of its French name, "SI") is built on seven key metrics, each based on a constant of physics: the second of time, the meter of extent, the kilogram of weight, the degree (Kelvin) of absolute temperature, the ampere of electrical current, the mole of molecular mass, and the candela of luminosity. On these foundations of mutual immutability is erected most of the machinery of global trade and commerce.[12]

These units of measure cannot float, because their constancy enables construction projects, computer designs, food processing gear, networks, refrigerators, fuels, pipelines, research laboratories, microchip capital equipment, industrial sensors, lighting systems, medical instruments, fiber optic cables, prosthetic devices, railroad tracks, storage facilities, hospital equipment, and other complex systems, in industry and government alike, to interconnect and function to keep us alive.

As Richard Vigilante puts it, "When baking a cake, we don't measure the flour against the sugar or the orange against the vanilla. We don't say we need two butters of bacon or three apples of orange. No, we use measuring cups and spoons from outside. We use measuring cups precisely because no one thinks the best use of a measuring cup is to bake it into the cake."[13]

Throughout most of human history, statesmen and philosophers alike have understood that money has a similar role. In the global economy, the currencies cannot be integrated with the commerce; they must have their roots in an absolute grid of measurement outside the process of exchange. If prices are uncoordinated, they will lead the business astray, and it will not add value to the economy. It will not produce knowledge through testable learning.

The SI metrics confirm that *time* is fundamental to all immutable and irreversible standards of measure. All but one of the seven key units directly resort to measurements constrained and defined, fixed and framed by physical constants governed by the passage of time. Thus the most fundamental of all the SI metrics is the *second*, which is determined by the speed of light in a vacuum. The rest of the measurements all essentially derive from this basic time constant of the universe.

The *meter*, for example, might seem to be a measure of space, but the SI roots it in the distance traveled by light in a vacuum during a tiny fraction of a second (actually the nine gigahertz emissions of the ground state cesium atom). As a measure of absolute temperature, *degrees Kelvin* are a reflection of frequencies bounded by the passage of seconds. The *kilogram* is tied to Planck's quantum constant h, a universal unit used to convert quantum wave functions into joules per second and hence tied to the speed of light. *Amperes* are governed by electromagnetism rooted in frequencies per second. *Candelas* are also Hertzian phenomena ruled by cycles per second.

The only exception in the SI table proves the rule. *Moles* escape a direct reference to time by being calculated by the Avogadro constant. But masses—and energies—as Einstein taught us, are also finally expressions of the speed of light in the lordly latency of seconds.

Money too, the key metric and information bearer in economics, is reliable only to the extent that its value is rooted in time. As the only irreversible element in the universe, with directionality imparted by thermodynamic entropy, time is the purest of reference points for all values.

Contemplating a new system of the world begetting new forms of money, governments and central banks are now feverishly trying to prove the effectiveness of their manipulations, their inflations and devaluations, their asset-buying splurges, and their redistributive potlatches.

These efforts to resist and divert the irreversible flows of time and entropy are sure to fail. Governments and central banks do not even control their own moneys. Quantitative tides of purchasing media are feckless before the choices of citizens who decide when to spend or invest any funds they command. Velocity and frequency trump the spurious time manipulations of the Keynesian regime.

In order to overcome the current economic doldrums afflicting the world, we must return to a regime of real money, anchored not in the caprices of bankers but in the physical constants of the universe.

Chapter 14

Restoring Real Money

I am more convinced than ever that if we ever again are going to have sound money it will not come from government. It will be issued by private enterprise.

—Friedrich Hayek, 1977[1]

C an we retrieve the American Dream? Can we unleash Silicon Valley, revive Main Street opportunities, and restore Wall Street to its crucial role in capitalizing innovation?

The answer is yes. An information economy is an economy of mind; it can be changed as fast as minds can change. Money is not a mystery. We, the people, can master it and make it our servant. The government monopoly on it can be ended tomorrow.

Although most economists believe in the intractability of existing conditions, whether it was the inflation of the 1970s or the stagnation of today, a reversal of policy can effect massive improvements in days and weeks. In the same way that existing policies suppress growth, a change in policy can bring about an instant and sharp enhancement of all entrepreneurial assets. Real money, lower tax rates, and deregulation can open up and lengthen the time horizons of enterprise.

Such transformations have happened in many different times and places. After World War II, for example, when ten million demobilized servicemen returned from the front to an economy that had to be converted from a garrison state to meet civilian needs, economists steeled themselves for a renewed great depression. But a big Republican victory in the elections of 1946 propelled a drastic turn away from the government-planning regime of the war, and President Harry Truman generally failed to resist the change.

Government spending plummeted by no less than 61 percent between 1945 and 1947. The economist Arnold Kling of the Cato Institute observes that "as a percentage of GDP the decrease in government purchases was larger than would result from the total elimination of government today."[2] Some 150,000 government regulators were laid off, along with perhaps a million other civilian employees of government. Disbanded were such managerial agencies as the War Production Board, the War Labor Board, and the Office of Price Administration, beloved of John Kenneth Galbraith.

Every Keynesian and socialist economist confidently predicted doom. In 1945, Paul Samuelson—sounding like his Nobel laureate successor Paul Krugman crying for trillions in new "stimulus," or Larry Summers predicting "secular stagnation," or Thomas Piketty and Robert Gordon envisioning an end to growth—prophesied "the greatest period of unemployment and dislocation which any economy has ever faced."

There was no new depression, though, and the historic ascent of America saved the world economy from socialism. Economic growth surged by 10 percent over two years. The civilian labor force expanded by seven million workers. Released from wartime controls, the private sector launched a ten-year boom despite tax rates on investors as high as 91 percent. Compensating for the high top rates was an effective 50 percent tax cut through the enactment of the joint return for households. Released from regulations and tax burdens and freed from wartime stresses, large manufacturing corporations emerged as spearheads of global capitalism.

Crucially complementing these deregulatory policies was an era of relatively sound and reliable money. The framework for this worldwide ascent from depression and war was the *gold exchange standard*. Negotiated in 1944 among all the Allied Powers at Bretton Woods, it made currencies convertible into dollars, which in turn were convertible into gold at thirty-five dollars an ounce.

The fixed exchange rates of Bretton Woods provided the stability that lengthened the horizons of global investment and enterprise. Remaining in place throughout the postwar boom, they provided the monetary backing for global growth that averaged 2.8 percent per year for twenty-five years, a level unequaled before or since and almost double the growth rate since 1971. There were few defaults, no banking crises, and an efflorescence of innovation and progress in what even current prophets of "secular stagnation" regard as a golden age.[3]

After the end of Bretton Woods, in 1971, the monetary regime became mostly dependent on the politics of central banking, chiefly the U.S. Federal Reserve and the European Central Bank. Although the dollar provided an adequate haven for extended periods, reliable money became increasingly scarce.

Nonetheless, by dismantling onerous controls and confiscatory tax rates, bold policy-makers still could work miracles of growth almost overnight.

New Zealand, once among the world's richest countries, with flourishing trade in agriculture and building materials, found itself sunk in socialist stagnation in the mid-1980s. Unable even to feed itself after twenty years of massive agricultural subsidies and supports, the country slipped into third-world conditions. With a top income-tax rate of 66 percent and a government share of GDP of 45 percent, New Zealand was mired in a slough of decline and paralysis.

Surprisingly, the change in policy came from the election of a Labour government that adopted a policy of zero-base budgeting for all government departments. The government sold off its airlines, railways, airports, seaports, bus lines, banks, hotels, insurance firms, maritime insurance companies, radio spectrum, printing facilities, forests, and irrigation schemes and an array of other holdings. It abolished farm programs that in 1985 were supplying 45 percent of all agricultural income. The central bank was privatized, made independent of the government, and restricted to a role of containing inflation.

Maurice McTigue, a former minister of transportation, sums up the results: "A decade later, New Zealand had one of the most competitive economies in the developed world. The government share of GDP had fallen to 27 percent, unemployment was a healthy 3 percent, and the top tax rate was 30 percent."[4] Eliminated were taxes on capital gains, inheritances, and luxuries, and excise duties were removed. Revenues surged, and "the government went from 23 years of deficits to 17 years of surpluses and repaid most of the nation's debt."

With the abolition of farm subsidies, New Zealand became one of the world's most creative and profitable food exporters. The number of different dairy products it produced grew from a mere handful to some seventeen thousand, and it was so successful at exporting cheese and butter that Wisconsin's dairy industry accused it of unfair trading tactics.

At the same time as New Zealand's about-face in the mid-1980s, Israel made a similar transition from a socialist economy in crisis to private and deregulated free enterprise with a disciplined monetary regime.[5] Allegedly complicating the Israeli challenge was the arrival of close to a million Russian Jews, many of them possessing advanced educational degrees and mathematical and engineering skills.

Israel benefited, as did the United States and New Zealand, from a dramatic change in political leadership and a new attitude toward enterprise. The conservative Likud Party, which took office in 1985, practiced pro-enterprise evangelism, cutting tax rates by 30 percent and shrinking the state-owned portion of Israel's leading corporations from 80 percent to 20 percent. Within a decade, Israel went from being a crippled industrial laggard, with inflation spiking as high as 1000 percent in 1984, to leading the world in per capita innovation and growth. Israel's creativity now animates many of the most powerful or popular American products, from Google traffic guidance to Apple iPhones, from the Internet to the medical center, from antimissile defenses to the ascendant realms of "cloud computing." Like America's postwar turnaround and New Zealand's transformation in the 1980s, the Israeli revival was an almost immediate response to a change in the economy of mind rather than in material conditions.

Perhaps most relevant today are the monetary lessons of the Chinese miracle. The laws of sound money and supply-side economics are so powerful that, under Mao's authoritarian but procapitalist successors, they transformed an economic wasteland into the world's largest and fastest-growing economy. Defying the monetarist counsel of Milton Friedman and the monetary harassment of four American presidents for alleged "manipulation," China accomplished this miracle by fixing its currency to the dollar. Its monetary conditions weren't perfect, but they were good enough, during decades of the dollar's relative stability, for a spectacular ascent of manufacturing.

Unfortunately, the United States in recent years has been engaged in supply-side suffocation, piling up oppressive regulations on manufacturing, industrial innovation, initial public offerings, and skilled immigration. A high-entropy government provides constant downside surprises of taxation, currency changes, and multifarious regulation, leaving low-entropy, low-profit residues for real private entrepreneurs.

U.S. policy has been so hostile to the private economy that a change could release enormous energy, discrediting once again the Keynesian and monetarist pessimists and galvanizing an American century. To accomplish this, we must abandon the idea that gushes of government funds can be converted into wealth. We must defer to the immemorial laws of money, recognizing again the flaws of monetarism—what money is and what it is not.

Based on *time*, real money is scarce, valuable, irreversible, and governed by entropy. It can be used to prioritize all the trade-offs and accounts of entrepreneurial life. Without time constraints, anything seems possible, particularly in the reality-distortion fields of government power. Money imposes time limits on enterprise and restrictions on government power. Real money brings reality to economic life.

By mutilating the rigorous time relations of money, politicians or central banks halt learning and shrink the time horizons of our lives. "Flash boys" trading in milliseconds do not refine the market, they merely oscillate it. Meaningless oscillation may yield "profits," but it does not produce learning. Thus it represents merely another way of asymptotically zeroing out time as the reality principle in economics.

In the past, the critique of monopoly money has taken the form of proposals for conferences, balanced budget amendments to the Constitution, and audits of the Federal Reserve and calls for a new Bretton Woods agreement. At a time of crisis, these ideas, however appealing, seem either trivial or implausible.

Most of the critics of monetary policy remain trapped by an idiom of runaway prices: dollar debauchery, fiat money devaluation, Weimar hyperinflation, the reversion of paper currencies to their intrinsic worth as confetti. Every year we are told to expect another interest-rate spike, an abandonment of the dollar, a wild commodity boom, a stock market cataclysm, and a sky-high price of gold. And every year interest rates adhere to their historic lows, commodities slump, the stock market survives and even thrives, the dollar waxes ever more dominant, and the price of gold languishes.

But it is a monetarist delusion that no inflation means no problem. Money is not a mere manifestation of economic power; it is a crucial source of information. Only to the extent that its signals of value are reliable and true can it guide the learning curves of wealth creation.

Government control and manipulation is to money what the
Soviet newspaper *Pravda* was to truth. With *expected* inflation,
entrepreneurs can function reasonably well. Workers may even
find that their wages rise as fast as prices and their houses appreciate faster than their mortgage payments grow. Debtors can see
their debts devalued. Under a *predictable* deflation, where prices
are reliably sinking as a result of real value creation, entrepreneurs
and workers can flourish. When sinking prices reflect an expanding economy of learning curves, with ever cheaper and more
useful goods and services, everyone can thrive.

In the face of arbitrary and *unpredictable* gyrations of value,
however, all are helpless but the dependents of government.
Unexpected gyrations falsify money as a bearer of information.
They turn prudent debts into deadly burdens or bonds into
bonanzas, transform contracts into shakedowns, payrolls into
ponderous exactions, and pensions into confetti or Sisyphean
boulders.

Economies founder when monetary policies and institutions
serve as a mendacious cover for drastic redistributions of wealth,
larcenous raids on the future, lavish rewards for political cronies
and colleagues. Economies fail when in pursuit of ideological
chimeras, central banks eclipse and collapse the information
content of prices. In an epistemological morass of manipulable
money, anyone with a long-term investment or asset, a fixed goal
or visionary cause, deep pockets or commitments, a family or a
career, or even an enduring job or marriage or family home or
employment pension becomes a gull for the government.

Because of the buildup of mountains of debt and contingent
liabilities across the globe under the management of central banks,
there seems to be no direct legislative path to a gold standard

today. The Byzantine emperors of the world monetary system have already sold out the future many times. Quantitative easing—the direct manipulative intervention in securities markets, buying some and spurning others—has become routine. Inflation has become policy.

Under the guise of "inflation targeting," nearly every central bank has adopted an official resolve to depreciate the purchasing power of its currency. The entire world is adopting *Pravda* money. As Steve Forbes points out, "2% inflation [Fed Chairman Janet Yellen's target] is effectively a 2% tax hike, an increase in the cost of living."[6] How can that stimulate the economy?

Even Larry Parks of the Foundation for the Advancement of Monetary Education has written, "Promulgating the gold standard today is the monetary equivalent of the 'Charge of the Light Brigade': defeat is assured. For every gold standard proponent— almost all of whom are not credentialed—there are hundreds of fully credentialed (with prizes, doctorates, endowed chairs, books, department headships, published peer-reviewed papers) 'expert' naysayers who will drown him out."

This should not be a counsel of despair. Even if the nation cannot forcibly impose a new gold standard on the world, real money is not an arbitrary legal structure or policy. It is an expression of the natural order of the economy, the system of the world. Since existing moneys fail to perform the key role of money as a measuring stick, we currently live in a world without money. What people call money is actually mere credit and debt with no reliable unit of account. A new gold standard will emerge when governments end their monopoly and remove obstructive taxes on alternative currencies. Allowed to move experimentally toward the time constraints of real money, digital payment systems will evolve with gold into a new information system for the global economy.

Critics of a gold standard fear it would restrict the money supply. But a gold standard does not fix the amount of money; it defines its value. Thus gold does not reduce the supply of real money. It increases the demand for it. Under the gold standard in the United States between 1775 and 1900, the money supply rose faster than at any time before or since—by a factor of 160—while the population rose by a factor of twenty-five and the nation forged its Industrial Revolution. This 160-fold rise in the real money supply, moreover, produced almost no inflation.

A gold standard complemented by bitcoin-related technologies on the Internet would provide a supply of real money for the first time since 1971. Gold enables real money by fixing its value to the passage of time. The supply is then determined by us, by private economic activity and learning based on the informative webs of authentic price signals.

Gold already serves as a monetary metric for millions of people around the globe. From China and India to the Middle Eastern oil kingdoms, many nations are increasing their stores of gold. Scores of entrepreneurs and venture capitalists are tapping gold's potential in international commerce. The Gold Standard Clearing House has experimentally reduced transaction times to under a hundred milliseconds. From Anthem Vault to Bitgold, entrepreneurs are developing ingenious combinations of the bitcoin blockchain with gold backing. Information technology and globalization are transforming the possibilities for new forms of money.

The most powerful corporations in the world, from Apple and Sony to Lenovo and Huawei, from Samsung and BASF to

ExxonMobil and Shell, are platform companies that express national cultures but operate everywhere. For such companies, floating currencies are increasingly costly and inconvenient. As a result, most of the overseas profits of leading U.S. multinationals, some $3 trillion, never reaches the United States. In addition, some fifty trillion of the dollar reserves of the world economy repose in the hands of Asian and Middle Eastern regimes skeptical toward the Western hostility to gold.

The goal of sound-money advocates should be to open a parallel path for international moneys that can both spur international trade and exchange and afford backup for the world economy in case of further turmoil. The multinational leviathans are increasingly seeking ways to circumvent national currencies and exactions. As time passes the world is evolving toward such a solution.

A first step in the United States would be removal of the capital gains tax on currencies. This country already allows gold currency. The Treasury mints millions of one-ounce silver eagle dollars that are worth more than twenty dollars apiece and one-ounce gold eagle fifty-dollar pieces that are worth $1,150 apiece. Virtually all these are hoarded. Though it has been legal since 1987 to use them at their metallic value, that route leads to a capital gains tax on their appreciation. Since the appreciation of a gold or silver piece is by reasonable definition all inflation, the tax is simple confiscation (like all capital gains taxes on spurious inflationary profits). The move of gold and silver coins into circulation would offer a corrective of constitutional money for any dollar debauchery by the Fed.

A key second step would be removal of the obstacles to alternative moneys on the Internet. Despite imprudent governmental interference in this planetary utility, it remains a bastion of American power, with U.S. companies such as Apple, Google, Amazon, Microsoft, Facebook, eBay, Cisco, Qualcomm, and scores of others capturing the bulk of all Internet revenues.

The Internet plays a central role in the American economy. But there is a profound flaw in its architecture. Its software stack lacks a trust and transactions capability. Its OSI (open systems interconnection) model defines seven layers (including the physical layer, the data link layer, the network layer, the transport layer, the session layer, the presentation layer, and the application layer). While some of the layers have merged, none of the existing layers provides trust or validation or factuality or veracity of real monetary values.

The Internet today desperately needs a new payment method that conforms to the shape and reach of global networking and commerce. It should obviate the constant exchanges of floating currencies, more volatile than the global economy that they supposedly measure. The new system should be distributed as far as Internet devices are distributed: a dispersed heterarchy based on peer-to-peer links between users rather than a centralized hierarchy based on national financial institutions. It should provide an automated system that benefits from Moore's and Metcalfe's learning curves to become more efficient with scale and capable of transactions of all sizes.[7] It should partake of the same monetary sources of stable value that characterize gold.

Fortunately such a payment system has already been invented. It is set to become a new facet of Internet infrastructure. It is called the bitcoin blockchain. It is already in place. It functions peer-to-peer without outside trusted third parties, and it follows Nick Szabo's precursor, bitgold. Its value, like gold's, is ultimately based on the scarcity of time. With automation it will become capable of micropayments. Even if bitcoin proves flawed, scores of companies are developing alternatives based on the essential blockchain innovation that can serve as a successful transactions layer for digital commerce.

The existence of such a system would enable sellers on the Internet, such as content producers, to name their own prices and collect their funds directly. And the very process that validates the transaction would prohibit spam. There would be no hassle of bartering content for advertising revenues at some aggregator such as Google. Aggregators with advertising clout would merely add inefficiency to an automated system that rides a learning curve to minimize transaction costs. The Internet would have a money system of its own with a granularity commensurate with its huge variety and with the many gradations of value transacted as an Internet user.

With a low market price for goods and services—Google and other players could charge millicents for their services and still make a mint—the Internet economy would transcend its current den of thieves and hustlers of spuriously free goods. It could attain its promise as a frictionless facilitator of human creativity rather than as a channel of chicanery. Its markets would impel the world along learning curves of growth toward new realms of knowledge and wealth.

But the success of a new global standard of value on the Internet entails a ban on taxation of Internet currencies. If only government moneys escape taxation, alternative currencies such as bitcoin will always be relegated to niches. Anyone serious about the reform of money must start by eliminating government obstruction of actual money.

A further step, as the monetary scholar Judy Shelton has advocated, is to "fix the dollar."[8] Her chief instrument would be the creation of Treasury Trust Bonds—five-year Treasuries redeemable in either dollars or gold. They could be enacted either through legislation or as a Treasury initiative.

> Legislation would specifically authorize the issuance of five-year Treasury securities that pay no interest but provide for payment of principal at maturity in either ounces of gold or the face value of the security, at the option of the holder. The instrument [would be] an obligation of the U.S. government to redeem the nominal value ("face value") in terms of a precise weight of gold stipulated in advance or the dollar amount established as the monetary equivalent. The rate of convertibility [in gold grams] is permanent throughout the life of the bond; it defines the gold value of the dollar.[9]

As Alan Greenspan declared in the *Wall Street Journal* during the previous era of monetary turmoil, in 1981:

> In years past a desire to return to a monetary system based on gold was perceived as nostalgia for an era when times were simpler, problems less complex and the world not threatened with nuclear annihilation. But after a decade of destabilizing inflation and economic stagnation, the restoration of a gold standard has become an issue that is clearly rising on the economic policy agenda.[10]

Greenspan suggested the path to the future through the creation of what now might be called "Shelton bonds": five-year Treasury notes payable in gold. "The degree of success of restoring long-term fiscal confidence," he argued, "will show up clearly in the yield spreads between gold and fiat dollar obligations of the same maturities." He concluded on a hopeful note: "Full convertibility would require that the yield spread for all maturities virtually disappear."

As Fed chairman, Greenspan went on to become a major maestro of monopoly money at the Fed. And in his subsequent books he expressed many regrets and misgivings about the nature and role of central banks. But in an era of new monetary turmoil, Shelton bonds still have traction: "An instrument that embodies a commitment to maintain the value of the dollar in terms of constant purchasing power will function as a barometer on the credibility of the Fed's eventual exit strategy from its lengthy and large-scale easing operations."

As bitcoin blockchain innovations spread through the Internet, borrowers could also issue bonds with a bitcoin payoff. As the price of gold and digital currencies converge on their common foundation of time, these real monies could ultimately redeem the dollar and the global economy.

New systems based on gold and blockchain innovations can evolve into a new world monetary infrastructure. Rooted in time, governed by entropy, intrinsically scarce, and always reliable, the money of the future can provide for a true global economy of knowledge and learning. Springing from the same information theory that is the basis of American enterprise, the new global money could extend the American Dream of stability and futurity.

The prophets of despair, posing as economic wizards, do not have the last word. We do. Restoring real money, we can recapture the future for both Silicon Valley and Wall Street. Opening up the horizons of opportunity again, we can save Main Street from the menace of monopoly money, transcending the dismal science of stagnation and decline and regaining the American mission and dream.

Acknowledgments

This book sprang from a monograph that I wrote as a fellow for the American Principles Project and continues my researches on money for APP under the patient and insightful guidance of Sean Fieler, Maggie Gallagher, and Richard Vigilante. It is based on the information theory of capitalism I expounded in *Knowledge and Power* and developed during some twenty years of studies in information theory at the Discovery Institute in Seattle, where I serve as a founding fellow. My editor at Regnery, Tom Spence, helped shape my ramshackle manuscript into the sleek and pithy text that you are now reading.

Key Terms for the Information Theory of Money

A Disordered Glossary of Counterintuitive Truths

Monopoly money: Money issued by sovereign states that block all competitive moneys in their domains, whether by regulation or by taxes not imposed on the sovereign currency. It's what we have in America and the rest of the world. Friedrich Hayek, the author of *The Road to Serfdom*, declared that "the source and root of all monetary evil [is] the government monopoly on the issue and control of money." Like most state-run monopolies, the money monopoly serves the interests of politicians rather than entrepreneurs, power rather than knowledge, old wealth rather than new ideas. Gold and bitcoin are the chief alternatives to monopoly money.

Hypertrophy of finance: The growth of finance beyond the rate of growth of the commerce it intermediates. For example, international currency trading is seventy-three times more voluminous than all global trading in goods and services and an estimated one hundred times as voluminous as all stock market transactions. Oil futures trading has risen by a factor of one hundred in some three decades, from 10 *percent* of oil output in 1984 to ten *times* oil output in 2015. Derivatives on real estate are now nine times global GDP. That's not capitalism, that's hypertrophy of finance.

Information theory: Based on the mathematical theories of Claude Shannon and Alan Turing, an evolving discipline that depicts human creations and communications as transmissions across a channel, whether that channel is a wire or the world. Measuring the outcome is its "news" or surprise, defined as entropy and consummated as knowledge.

Entropy is higher or lower depending on the freedom of choice of the sender. The larger the available alphabet of symbols—that is, the larger the set of possible messages—the greater the composer's choice and the higher the entropy and information of the message.

Since these creations and communications can be business plans or experiments, information theory provides the foundation for an economics driven not by equilibrium or order but by falsifiable entrepreneurial surprises.

Information theory both enables and describes our digital world.

Noise: Distortion of content by its conduit. A high-entropy message (full of surprise) requires a low-entropy channel (with no surprises). Surprises in the signal are information; surprises in the channel are noise.

Wealth: Tested knowledge. Physical law dictates that matter is conserved: material resources have not changed since the Stone Age. All enduring economic advances come from the increase of knowledge through *learning*.

Economic growth: *Learning* tested by falsifiability or possible bankruptcy. This understanding of economic growth follows from Karl Popper's insight that a scientific proposition must be framed in terms that are falsifiable or refutable. Government guarantees prevent learning and thus thwart economic growth.

All expanding businesses and industries follow a *learning curve* that ordains a 20 to 30 percent decrease in costs with every doubling of total units sold. Classical learning curves are MOORE's LAW in SILICON VALLEY and METCALFE's LAW in networking. Raymond Kurzweil generalized the concept as a "law of accelerating returns."

Moore's Law: Cost-effectiveness in the computer industry doubles every two years. This pace corresponds closely to a faster pace in the number of transistors produced, signifying a learning curve. Formulated by Intel founder Gordon Moore and inspired by Caltech professor Carver Mead's research, Moore's Law was originally based on the biennial doubling of the density of transistors on a silicon chip. It now chiefly relies on other vectors of innovation, such as parallel processing, multi-threading, lower voltages, and three-dimensional chip architectures. Moore's Law has become an important principle of INFORMATION THEORY.

Metcalfe's Law: The value and power of a network grows by the square of the number of compatible nodes it links. Named for the engineer Robert Metcalfe, a co-inventor of Ethernet, this law is a rough index and deeply counterintuitive. (It would be preposterous to claim that the Internet is worth the square of its six billion connected devices.) But the law applies to smaller networks, and it explains the vectors of value creation of companies such as Facebook, Apple, Google, and Amazon, which now dominate stock market capitalization. Metcalfe's Law may well apply to the promise of new digital currencies and ultimately assure the success of a new transactions layer for the Internet software stack.

Wall Street: The symbol of the financial industry, from investment banks to insurance companies, from credit card vendors to payday lenders, from brokers to hedge funds. Today Wall Street is gorging itself on the HYPERTROPHY OF FINANCE. Ideally, finance *intermediates* transactions across time through interest rates and across space through currency-exchange rates. But today both these functions are falsified by government manipulation. They face *dis*intermediation by gold, by a new transactions layer in the Internet software stack, and by new cryptographic blockchain currencies. In the hypertrophy of finance, Wall Street was bloated by MONOPOLY MONEY created by the Federal Reserve and channeled to the U.S. Treasury by banks, never touching MAIN STREET.

Main Street: The symbol of the real economy of workers paid hourly or monthly and sealed off from the circular loops of WALL STREET moneymaking. Perhaps the street where you live, Main Street is the site of local businesses and jobs.

Silicon Valley: A symbol of the high-tech entrepreneurial economy, centered in Santa Clara County, California, and largely funded by venture capital from SAND HILL ROAD in Palo Alto and Menlo Park. The high-tech economy is increasingly based on INFORMA-TION THEORY, which governs its infrastructure of communications and computing, particularly software. Silicon Valley sustains both MAIN STREET and WALL STREET by supplying them with new technology. Through Wall Street, Silicon Valley provides Main Street with opportunities for sharing in the equity of the ascendant sectors of the world economy.

In recent years, Silicon Valley has suffered from the HYPER-TROPHY OF FINANCE, become bloated with MONOPOLY MONEY, and been bent by controls from the Wall Street–Washington axis. Like Wall Street, Silicon Valley has bypassed Main Street, which has remained trapped in its pedestrian time-based compensation and mindless index fund investments.

Sand Hill Road: The arboreal abode of California venture capitalists and their "unicorns," stretching from the Camino Real near Stanford to Route 280 and into the clouds and wealth of Woodside and SILICON VALLEY.

Expansionary fiscal and monetary policy: The attempt by central banks to stimulate economic activity by selling government securities to pay for a governmental deficit. Keynesians believe that selling securities will impart a fiscal stimulus by enabling more government spending.

Monetarists, on the other hand, believe that to stimulate economic activity central banks should create money to *buy* government securities, money that supposedly is put into the economy. But this new money goes to the owners of the purchased securities, chiefly banks, which in recent years have used their money to purchase more securities from the Treasury. Thus Keynesianism and monetarism converge in expanding the government's power to spend.

In an information economy, both measures attempt to use government power to force growth. But ECONOMIC GROWTH is *learning* (accumulating tested knowledge). Learning cannot be forced.

Real money: A measuring stick, a metric of value, reflecting the scarcity and irreversible passage of time—entropy based, equally distributed, and founded on the physical limits of the speed of light and the span of life. BITCOIN and GOLD are both real money in this sense. MONOPOLY MONEY is not.

Bitcoin blockchain: A method of secure transactions based on wide publication and decentralization of a ledger across the Internet, in contrast to current credit card systems based on secrecy and centralization, using protected networks and firewalled data centers filled with the personal information of the transactors.

The public ledger of transactions is collected in blocks roughly every ten minutes, beginning with the current block and going back to the "Genesis block" created by Satoshi Nakamoto, the pseudonymous inventor of bitcoin. Each block is confirmed when at least half the participants in bitcoin nodes—the "miners"— hash the block mathematically with all the previous blocks since the Genesis block. In order to change or rescind a transaction, therefore, more than half the computers in the system have to agree to recompute and restate all the transactions since Genesis.

Bitcoins are used to evaluate transactions based on the time taken to validate a block. Bitcoins thus are not coins but metrics or measuring sticks for transactions that are permanently registered in the BLOCKCHAIN.

Blockchain: A database, similar to a cadastre of real estate titles, extended to events, covenants, patents, licenses, or other permanent records. All are hashed together mathematically from the origin of the series, with the record distributed and publicized on decentralized Internet nodes.

Gold: The monetary element, tested over centuries. Usually thought to be money because it is a useful commodity—pretty, shiny, divisible, portable, scarce, and convertible into jewelry— gold is in fact the monetary element because it is useless. Money is not valuable because it is really jewelry; jewelry is valuable because it is really money. Gold is a metric of valuation based on the time to extract an incremental ounce, which has changed little over the centuries while gold has become more difficult to extract from deeper and more-attenuated lodes.

Shannon entropy: Information measured by surprisal, or unexpected bits, "news." Counterintuitively, surprising information is a kind of disorder. The alphabet is ordered; crystals are ordered; snowflakes are ordered. *Hamlet* and Google are beautifully disordered alphabets conveying surprising information.

Physical entropy (a.k.a. Boltzmann's entropy): Disorder. In a system divided between hot and cold entities, Boltzmann's entropy begins as zero—when we know most about the arrangement of the system—and it reaches maximum entropy when those hot and cold entities merge and we know least. Boltzmann therefore identified entropy with missing information, or uncertainty about the arrangement of the molecules, opening the way for Shannon and INFORMATION THEORY.

Although the Boltzmann and Shannon equations are similar, Boltzmann's entropy is analog and governed by the natural logarithm, e. Shannon entropy is digital and governed by the binary logarithm, log base 2.

Gödel's incompleteness theorem: Every logical system depends on propositions outside the system that are unprovable within the system. The first person to appreciate and publicize the importance of Kurt Gödel's demonstration in 1931 that mathematical statements can be true but unprovable was John von Neumann.

As von Neumann saw, Gödel's proof depended on his invention of a mathematical "machine" that used numbers to encode and prove algorithms also expressed in numbers. This invention, absorbed by von Neumann and Alan Turing, launched computer science and INFORMATION THEORY and enabled the development of the Internet and the BLOCKCHAIN.

Notes

PROLOGUE: WINNING THE DEBATE

1. Robert L. Bartley, *The Seven Fat Years, and How to Do It Again* (New York, NY: The Free Press, 1992).

2. Robert J. Samuelson, "The Startup Slump," *Washington Post*, December 22, 2015. Citing a National Bureau of Economic Research paper, Samuelson reports a "double-whammy": a 37 percent decline in the proportion of start-ups—from 13 percent of all firms in the late 1980s to 8 percent in 2011—and a decline in their rate of growth to a level below the growth rate of older companies, which in turn have slowed their investment in new plants and equipment. He concludes, "Compared to the past, companies seem more reluctant to invest in the future."

3. Nassim Nicholas Taleb and Mark Spitznagel, in a blog post at CNN's *Global Public Square* from October 2012, estimate that

$2.2 trillion was paid to bankers, chiefly in bonuses, in the United States alone between June 2000 and June 2007, and they project the total to rise to (very roughly) $5 trillion over the course of the decade. "Bankers used leverage to increase profitability and exploited the backstop of public guarantees. The profits largely flow to the employees [i.e., the bankers], while the losses are defrayed by the taxpayers and shareholders and even retirees (through artificially low interest rates). The Fed also provided $1.2 trillion in loans to banks (mostly secret at the time)."

4. Carmen M. Reinhart and Kenneth Rogoff, *This Time Is Different: Eight Centuries of Financial Folly* (Princeton, NJ: Princeton University Press, 2011).

5. Mark Skousen, *Vienna & Chicago, Friends or Foes? A Tale of Two Schools of Free-Market Economics* (Washington, DC: Capital Press, 2005). Skousen superbly covers the canonical sources of Austrian and Chicago economic thought. See also Robert P. Murphy and Donald J. Boudreaux, *Choice: Cooperation, Enterprise and Human Action* (Oakland, CA: Independent Institute, 2015). For the definitive texts, see Ludwig von Mises, *Human Action*, and Friedrich Hayek, *The Road to Serfdom*, both available in many editions.

6. Daniel Kahneman, *Thinking, Fast and Slow* (New York, NY: Farrar, Straus and Giroux, 2011). The Israeli cognitive psychologist Amos Tversky was his collaborator.

CHAPTER ONE: THE DREAM AND THE DOLLAR

1. Louis Simpson, "In California," in *The Owner of the House: New Collected Poems, 1940–2001* (Rochester, NY: BOA Editions, 2003), 173.

2. "There was virtually no growth before 1750, and thus there is no guarantee that growth will continue indefinitely. Rather, the paper suggests that the rapid progress made over the past 250 years could well turn out to be a unique episode in human history." Robert J. Gordon, "Is U.S. Economic Growth Over? Faltering Innovation Confronts the Six Headwinds," working paper no. 18315, National Bureau of Economic Research, August 2012. In early 2016, Gordon expanded these themes into a widely touted and conscientious tome, *The Rise and Fall of American Growth: The U.S. Standard of Living Since the Civil War* (Princeton, NJ: Princeton University Press, 2016). Though full of intriguing insights, it finally founders on its mostly academic sources and becomes merely the most definitively and exhaustively mounted alibi for socialist slowdown. It frets about "inequality," "global warming," and other facets of spurious conventional wisdom, but fails to ascribe any role to monopoly money or to luddite control of the government and the academy.

3. Lawrence Summers, "Reflections on the Productivity Slowdown," keynote address, Peterson Institute for International Economics, Washington, DC, November 16, 2015. Summers here offers second thoughts about his earlier endorsement of the "secular stagnation" thesis. Now he asks how skilled labor and new technology could be displacing so many workers if productivity were not increasing. He also asked his audience how many would trade their healthcare in 2015 for the allegedly much cheaper healthcare in 1950. Since everyone refused the offer, Summers concludes that, adjusted for quality, healthcare has not risen in price. Thus productivity in healthcare has improved far more than the measured gains. See also Bret Swanson, "Moore's Law and the Productivity Paradox,"

AEIdeas (blog), November 25, 2015, https://www.aei.org/
publication/moores-law-and-the-productivity-paradox/.

4. Thomas Piketty, *Capital in the Twenty-First Century* (Cambridge,
    MA: Harvard University, Belknap Press, 2014).

5. Ta-Nehisi Coates, *Between the World and Me* (New York, NY:
    Spiegel and Grau, 2015). See also Kyle Smith, "The Hard Untruths
    of Ta-Nehisi Coates: A Bestselling Polemic Riven with Hatred
    Thrills the Liberal Elite," *Commentary*, October 2015, pp. 20–25.

6. Yuval Levin, "The Mobility Crisis," *Commentary*, March 2015,
    pp. 12–20.

7. Kwasi Kwarteng, *War and Gold: A 500-Year History of Empires,
    Adventures, and Debt* (New York, NY: PublicAffairs, 2014), 219–
    20.

8. Peter Thiel with Blake Masters, *Zero to One: Notes on Startups,
    or How to Build the Future* (New York, NY: Crown Business,
    2014), 5–11 and passim.

CHAPTER 2: JUSTICE BEFORE GROWTH

1. George Gilder, *Knowledge and Power: The Information Theory
    of Capitalism and How It Is Revolutionizing Our World*
    (Washington, DC: Regnery Publishing, 2013). See also Cesar
    Hidalgo, *Why Information Grows: The Evolution of Order from
    Atoms to Economics* (New York, NY: Basic Books, 2015). The
    MIT scholar offers a similar information theory of capitalism, with
    many ingenious refinements, that nonetheless goes astray from my
    point of view by identifying information with order. So does Matt
    Ridley, *The Evolution of Everything: How New Ideas Emerge*
    (New York, NY: HarperCollins, 2015). These brilliant men, ready
    to grasp ideas with prehensile mastery, come a cropper on the

counterintuitive findings of information theory. Information is not order but its opposite. Order is the low-entropy carrier that makes it possible to identify information (and complexity) as disorder. Both Hidalgo and Ridley imagine that there is a conflict between evolution and the second law of thermodynamics, the entropy law. But both complex systems and entropy represent surprising deformations of order.

2. "Costs and the Experience Curve, Why Costs Go Down Forever," chapter 2 of Bruce D. Henderson, *The Logic of Business Strategy* (Cambridge, MA: Ballinger Publishing, 1984), 47ff.

3. "The Six Epochs" and "The Law of Accelerating Returns," chapters 1 and 2 of Ray Kurzweil, *The Singularity Is Near* (New York, NY: Viking, 2005), 7–34.

4. William D. Nordhaus, "Do Real-Output and Real-Wage Measures Capture Reality? The History of Lighting Suggests Not," Cowles Foundation for Research in Economics at Yale University, 1998. This epochal paper was delivered first to the National Bureau of Economic Research in 1993. I first encountered it in David Warsh's definitive *Knowledge and the Wealth of Nations* (New York, NY: W. W. Norton, 2007), 336.

5. Nicholas Eberstadt, "How the World Is Becoming More Equal," *Wall Street Journal*, August 26, 2014. Eberstadt documents that globally life spans have never been so long and evenly distributed, with even China now reaching an average of longer than seventy years.

6. Thomas Sowell, "Income Distribution," *The Thomas Sowell Reader* (New York, NY: Basic Books, 2011), 98–107.

7. Charles Gave, "Of Wicksell and Fed Fallacies," Gavekal Research, September 4, 2014, p. 4.

CHAPTER 3: FRIEDMAN AND THE ENIGMA OF MONEY

1. Ronald I. McKinnon, *Money and Capital in Economic Development* (Washington, DC: Brookings Institution, 1973).

2. Milton Friedman, *Capitalism and Freedom* (Chicago, IL: University of Chicago Press, 1962); and Friedman, *Free to Choose* (New York, NY: Harcourt, 1980).

3. Economists tend to restrict velocity to GDP over the money supply, as if the public only contributed to "demand" by purchasing final products in GDP. But the public can also invest, speculate, or collect, and these actions are if anything more significant than mere spending.

4. "Gross Output provides an important new perspective on the economy; and one that is closer to the way many businesses see themselves," says Steve Landefeld, director of the Bureau of Economic Analysis. The government began releasing this statistic in the spring of 2014. GDP measures the "use" economy, final goods and services, from grande lattes to automobiles to residential housing. GO includes the "make" economy—all the intermediate production of components and commodities that preceded the final sale. Although GO may seem to double count, adding the steel and plastic in the car to the final sale of the automobile, GDP arbitrarily treats human beings merely as final consumers of goods like food and fuel. Their more important role in the economy is as workers and producers using food and fuel to sustain themselves as producers of new goods and services, knowledge and learning.

5. "Monetary Rules Work and Discretion Doesn't," chapter 1 in John B. Taylor, *First Principles: Five Keys to Restoring America's Prosperity* (New York, NY: W. W. Norton, 2012).

6. Ramesh Ponnuru and David Beckworth, "The Right Goal for Central Banks," *National Review*, June 11, 2012, p. 36.

7. "Should We Worry about US Velocity?," chapter 9 in Louis-Vincent Gave, *Too Different for Comfort* (Hong Kong: Gavekal Books, 2014). See also Charles Gave, "A Fisherian Take on Velocity," Gavekal Research, October 11, 2013.

8. Louis-Vincent Gave, *Too Different for Comfort*, 49.

9. Lewis Lehrman, "Jacques Rueff, the Age of Inflation, and the True Gold Standard," speech, Assemble Nationale, November 7, 1996. See also Lehrman, *Money, Gold and History* (New York, NY: Lehrman Institute, 2013), 147. Lehrman has been the single most persistent and resourceful advocate of what he terms the "true gold standard" in his book by that name: *True Gold Standard* (New York, NY: Lehrman Institute, 2012). He quotes Keynes, who in 1922 declared: "If the gold standard could be reintroduced...we all believe that the reform would promote trade and production like nothing else, but also stimulate international credit and transfers of capital to where they are the most useful. One of the greatest elements of uncertainty would be suppressed."

10. Milton Friedman, interview in the *Financial Times*, San Francisco, CA, June 28, 2003.

CHAPTER 4: THE CHINESE CHALLENGE

1. David Stockman, "The Great China Ponzi—an Economic and Financial Trainwreck Which Will Rattle the World," David Stockman's Contra Corner, August 16, 2015, http://davidstockmanscontracorner.com/the-great-china-ponzi-an-economic-and-financial-trainwreck-which-will-rattle-the-world/; and Stockman, "China's Monumental Ponzi: Here's How It Unravels," David Stockman's Contra Corner, March 31, 2014, http://davidstockmanscontracorner.com/chinas-monumental-ponzi-heres-how-it-unravels/.

2.   George Gilder, "Let a Billion Flowers Bloom," in David Boaz, ed., *Toward Liberty: The Idea That Is Changing the World* (Washington, DC: Cato Institute, 2002), 180–81.

3.   Purchasing power parity calculations, widely criticized as inaccurate, showed China as the largest economy in 2014, though by per capita standards the United States remained more than 40 percent ahead in 2015. In a world with no reliable monetary standard, purchasing power parity is the only way to compare different economies. Economists evidently agree that currency prices fail to gauge actual values.

4.   These statistics comparing foreign exchange market (forex) trading with total stock market and goods and services trade are calculated from the total of daily foreign exchange transactions published every three years by the Bank for International Settlements (BIS). This number is then compared to global international stock market trading and goods and services trade divided by the number of days. Kenichi Ohmae of McKinsey & Company wrote a book titled *The Borderless World* (New York, NY: HarperCollins, 1990) at a time when trading volume was $600 billion a *day*, compared with related goods and services trade of $600 billion *yearly*: "No one can argue that FX trading is still a mere adjunct to other forms of economic activity. It is an end in itself."

5.   "Twenty First Century Capitalism," chapter 17 in Nathan K. Lewis, *Gold: The Monetary Polaris* (New Berlin, NY: Canyon Maple Publishing, 2013), 271–80.

6.   "Estimates by several analysts show that China's gold imports are heading for an annual total of close to 2,100 tonnes" compared to previous leader India's 1000 tons. Taki Tsaklanos, "China and India Hoarding Massive Amounts of Gold," *Financial Sense*, January 18, 2015.

7. Stockman, "The Great China Ponzi."

8. Charles Gave et al., *Our Brave New World* (Hong Kong: Gavekal Research, 2005), 74 and passim. Since 2005, Chinese urban incomes have soared again.

CHAPTER 5: THE HIGH COSTS OF BAD MONEY

1. Peter Schiff, *The Real Crash: America's Coming Bankruptcy* (New York, NY: St. Martin's Press, 2012).

2. Eswar S. Prasad, *The Dollar Trap: How the U.S. Dollar Tightened Its Grip on Global Finance* (Princeton, NJ: Princeton University Press, 2014), 18 and passim.

3. Paul Krugman, *End This Depression Now* (New York, NY: W. W. Norton, 2012).

4. Ibid.

5. Ibid.

6. Robert J. Gordon, "Is U.S. Economic Growth Over? Faltering Innovation Confronts the Six Headwinds," working paper no. 18315, National Bureau of Economic Research, August 2012. See also Lawrence Summers, "U.S. Economic Prospects: Secular Stagnation, Hysteresis, and the Zero Lower Bound," keynote address, National Association of Business Economists' Policy Conference, February 24, 2014, which focuses on the impotence of expansionary monetary policy when interest rates approach zero.

7. Peter Thiel with Blake Masters, *Zero to One: Notes on Startups, or How to Build the Future* (New York, NY: Crown Business, 2014), 193. For my time-sensitive money, this is the most original and interesting book ever written on business strategy. (Its chief rival is the more technical *Innovators' Dilemma* by Clayton Christensen).

8.   Nassim Nicholas Taleb and Mark Spitznagel, "The Great Bank Robbery," *Global Public Square*, CNN, October 2011.

9.   David Malpass, speech to the Needham Growth Conference, New York, January 15, 2015. As Malpass points out, zero interest rates mean free money, and "when anything is free it is allocated by queue and only the privileged folk at the front of the line get any."

10.   Charles Gave, "Poverty Matters for Capitalists," GavekalDragonomics (Hong Kong: Gavekal Global Research, July 9, 2014), 1–6.

CHAPTER 6: MONEY IN INFORMATION THEORY

1.   Michael Lewis, *Flash Boys: A Wall Street Revolt* (New York, NY: W. W. Norton, 2014).

2.   Sir John Craig, *The Mint* (Cambridge: Cambridge University Press, 1953), 198 and passim.

3.   Nick Gillespie, "FreedomFest Interview with George Gilder," *ReasonTV*, August 12, 2014.

4.   These themes are the subject of *Knowledge and Power: The Information Theory of Capitalism and How It Is Revolutionizing Our World* (Washington, DC: Regnery, 2013).

5.   Kwasi Kwarteng, *War and Gold: A 500-Year History of Empires, Adventures, and Debt* (New York, NY: PublicAffairs, 2014), 361–62.

6.   "The World's Experience with Gold Standard Systems," chapter 5 in Nathan K. Lewis, *Gold: The Monetary Polaris* (New Berlin, NY: Canyon Maple Publishing, 2013).

7.   "How We Got Here," chapter 1 in Steve Forbes and Elizabeth Ames, *Money: How the Destruction of the Dollar Threatens the Global Economy—and What We Can Do about It* (New York, NY: McGraw Hill, 2014), 7–24.

8.   Lewis, *Gold*.

9.   Takashi Kiuchi, *The Terra TRC White Paper*, originally published
     February 27, 2004, and subsequently updated. These numbers are
     tabulated every three years by the Bank for International Settlements.

10. IDC Financial Insights, *Worldwide Banking IT Spending Guide*
     (Farmingham, MA: IDC Corporate USA).

11. "The United States' Experience with Gold Standard Systems,"
     chapter 3 in Lewis, *Gold*, 64–85.

CHAPTER 7: WHAT BITCOIN CAN TEACH

1.   "Twenty-First Century Capitalism," chapter 17 in Nathan K.
     Lewis, *Gold: The Monetary Polaris* (New Berlin, NY: Canyon
     Maple Publishing, 2013), 271–80.

2.   "E-Commerce Speeds Up, Hits Record High Share of Retail Sales,"
     MarketWatch (blog), August 15, 2014, http://blogs.marketwatch.
     com/capitolreport/2014/08/15/e-commerce-speeds-up-hits-record-
     high-share-of-retail-sales/.

3.   Susan Vranica, "The Secret about On-Line Ad Traffic, One-Third
     is Bogus," *Wall Street Journal*, March 23, 2014, http://www.wsj.
     com/articles/SB10001424052702304026304579453253860786
     62.

4.   Nick Szabo, "Macroscale Replicator," October 19, 1995.

5.   Szabo's blog, *Unenumerated*, is published online by Forbes.com.
     All the quotations here are from the *Unenumerated* archive.

6.   Richard Vigilante, personal communication.

CHAPTER 8: WHERE "HAYEKS" GO WRONG

1.   Ferdinando M. Ametrano, "Hayek Money: The Cryptocurrency
     Price Stability Solution," Social Science Research Network, revised
     July 5, 2015, http://ssrn.com/abstract=2425270, 54. Ametrano's
     paper was shortlisted as a finalist for the Blockchain Awards,

category Visionary Academic Paper, at the Bitcoin Foundation Conference 2014, but it lost to Nakamoto's original breakthrough paper.

2. Ibid., 5–6.

3. Ibid., 10.

4. Ibid., 20; and Friedrich A. Hayek, *Denationalization of Money— The Argument Refined*, 3rd ed. (London: The Institute of Economic Affairs, 1990).

5. Ametrano, "Hayek Money," 20.

6. Ametrano, presentation to the Central Bank of Italy, June 9, 2014.

7. George Gilder, *Telecosm: The World after Bandwidth Abundance* (New York, NY: Simon & Schuster, 2002).

8. Board of Governors of the Federal Reserve System, "Current FAQs: Informing the Public about the Federal Reserve," http://www. federalreserve.gov/faqs/faq.htm.

9. Richard Vigilante, personal communication.

10. Hayek, "A Free-Market Monetary System," lecture at the Gold and Monetary Conference, New Orleans, LA, November 10, 1977, *Journal of Libertarian Studies* 3, no. 1.

11. Satoshi Nakamoto, "Bitcoin: A Peer-to-Peer Electronic Cash System," Bitcoin.org, 2008.

12. George Sammon, speech to CoinAgenda, Las Vegas, October 2014.

CHAPTER 9: THE PIKETTY-TURNER THESIS

1. Thomas Piketty, *Capital in the Twenty-First Century* (Cambridge, MA: Harvard University, Belknap Press, 2014).

2. "The Scandal of Money," chapter 12 in George Gilder, *Knowledge and Power: The Information Theory of Capitalism and How It Is Revolutionizing Our World* (Washington, DC: Regnery Publishing, 2013), 113–23.

3. Adair Turner, *Between Debt and the Devil: Money, Credit, and Fixing Global Finance* (Princeton, NJ: Princeton University Press, 2016).

4. Joseph E. Stiglitz, *Globalization and Its Discontents* (New York, NY: W. W. Norton, 2002); and Paul Krugman, *The Return of Depression Economics and the Crisis of 2008* (New York, NY: W. W. Norton, 2013).

5. "I don't particularly feel like defending currency speculation. I consider it a necessary evil. *I think it is better than currency restrictions, but a unified currency would be even better* [my italics].... When speculators profit, the authorities have failed in some way or another. But they don't like to admit failure; they would rather call for speculators to be hung from lampposts than to engage in a little bit of soul searching to see what they did wrong." George Soros, *Soros on Soros: Staying Ahead of the Curve* (New York, NY: John Wiley & Sons, 1995).

6. Turner, *Between Debt and the Devil*, 19–20.

7. Henry George, *Progress and Poverty: An Inquiry into the Cause of Industrial Depressions and of Increase of Want with Increase of Wealth... The Remedy* (New York, NY: Robert Schalkenbach Foundation, 1979).

8. Turner, *Between Debt and the Devil*, 73, 176, 180.

CHAPTER 10: HYPERTROPHY OF FINANCE

1. Ronald McKinnon, *Money in International Exchange: The Convertible Currency System* (New York, NY: Oxford University Press, 1979), 3 and passim. Writing in 1978, just seven years after Nixon rescinded Bretton Woods, the Stanford economist showed that various currency cocktails, such as the International Monetary Fund's then-heralded "special drawing rights," could not address

any real monetary problems and that commodity baskets (whether "full bodied" or fractionally reserved) would serve no purpose either, despite their cumbersome and costly practicalities. He demonstrated convincingly that gold and the dollar are the real alternatives.

I emerged from this definitive early text with the belief that control of money as a key facet of sovereignty is a treacherous temptation, since "monetary policies" by definition create "noise" in the market. They use distortions of currency as a unit of account in order to hedge, spur, subsidize, or channel economic activity in directions favored by the government and banking sectors.

2. Commodity HQ, "Top 7 Buffett Quotes on Gold Investing," Minyanville, October 3, 2012, http://www.minyanville.com/trading-and-investing/commodities/articles/Warren-Buffett-brka-gold-investing-investing/10/3/2012/id/44617.

3. Christopher Shea, "Survey: No Support for Gold Standard among Top Economists," *Ideas Market* (blog), *Wall Street Journal*, January 23, 2012, http://blogs.wsj.com/ideas-market/2012/01/23/survey-no-support-for-gold-standard-among-top-economists/.

4. Milton Friedman and Anna Jacobson Schwartz, *A Monetary History of the United States, 1867–1960* (Princeton, NJ: Princeton University Press, 1963). See also "Reflections on a Monetary History," in *The Indispensable Milton Friedman: Essays on Politics and Economics*, Lanny Ebenstein, ed. (Washington, DC: Regnery, 2012), 229–32.

5. Ben Bernanke and Harold James, "The Gold Standard, Deflation, and Financial Crisis in the Great Depression: An International Comparison," in *Financial Markets and Financial Crises*, R. Glenn Hubbard, ed. (Chicago, IL: University of Chicago Press, 1991), 33–68.

6.   Walter B. Wriston, *The Twilight of Sovereignty: How the Information Revolution Is Transforming Our World* (New York, NY: Scribner, 1992; Replica Books, Lord and Taylor, Bridgewater, NJ: 1997), 9, 59–62, and passim. Wriston beat Thomas Friedman to all the crucial insights of *The World Is Flat* by fifteen years.

7.   Ibid., 9.

8.   "OTC Foreign Exchange Turnover by Instrument, Counterparty and Currency in April 2013, 'Net-Net' Basis, Total Reported Transactions in All Currencies," in Bank for International Settlements, *Triennial Central Bank Survey: Global Foreign Exchange Market Turnover in 2013* (Switzerland: 2014).

9.   Eric Janszen, *The Postcatastrophe Economy: Rebuilding America and Avoiding the Next Bubble* (New York, NY: Portfolio, 2010), 36ff.

CHAPTER 11: MAIN STREET PUSHED ASIDE

1.   Robert J. Samuelson, "Obama's Economic Choices Leaving His Successor Horrible Hurdles," *Washington Post*, September 14, 2015.

2.   Samuelson, "Remarkably, Fannie Mae and Freddie Mac's Importance Today Is Unparalleled," *Washington Post*, November 16, 2015.

3.   "[W]e...describe the economy as the system by which people accumulate knowledge and knowhow to create packets of physical order, or products, that augment our capacity to accumulate more knowledge and knowhow.... The finiteness of human beings and of the networks we form limits our ability to accumulate and transmit knowledge and knowhow, leading to spatial accumulations...that result in global inequality.... Silicon Valley's knowledge and knowhow are not contained in a collection of perennially

unemployed experts but rather in the experts working in firms that participate in the design and development of software and hardware." Cesar Hidalgo, *Why Information Grows: The Evolution of Order, from Atoms to Economies* (New York, NY: Basic Books, 2015), 8, 142, and passim.

4. Charles Gave et al., *Our Brave New World* (Hong Kong: Gavekal Research, 2005) offers the definitive exposition of the rising role and dominance of the "platform company" model.

5. Nick Bilton, "Is Silicon Valley in Another Tech Bubble?," *Vanity Fair*, September 2015.

6. Marc A. Miles, "The Fed's Zero Interest Rate Policies Amount to a War on Jobs," *Forbes*, June 4, 2013, http://www.forbes.com/sites/realspin/2013/06/04/the-feds-zero-interest-rate-policies-amount-to-a-war-on-jobs/#2715e4857a0b72333a807421.

7. David Malpass, "Pro-Growth Tools for the Frozen Fed," *Wall Street Journal*, October 6, 2015.

CHAPTER 12: WALL STREET SELLS ITS SOUL

1. Mike Konczal, "The Devastating Lifelong Consequences of Student Debt," *New Republic*, June 24, 2014. See also Bill Walton, *On Common Ground*, interview with George Gilder.

2. Peter Thiel with Blake Masters, *Zero to One: Notes on Startups, or How to Build the Future* (New York, NY: Crown Business, 2014), 89–90; and George Gilder, *Knowledge and Power: The Information Theory of Capitalism and How It Is Revolutionizing Our World* (Washington, DC: Regnery Publishing, 2013), 29–33. The figures on jobs contribution from venture capital vary from 11 percent to 17 percent, but since the epochs of slavery and socialism all jobs have stemmed from the process of knowledge accumulation and learning, which is the focus of venture investment.

3.   Charles Gave, "Indexation=Parasitism," GavekalDragonomics
      (Hong Kong: Gavekal Research, July 15, 2014), 1.

4.   John C. Bogle, *The Clash of Cultures: Investment vs. Speculation*
      (New York, NY: John Wiley and Sons, 2012). Bogle astonishingly
      sees the culture of investment as index funds and the culture of
      speculation as actively managed capital.

5.   Nassim Nicholas Taleb and Mark Spitznagel, blog post, *Global
      Public Square*, CNN, October 2012.

6.   Ibid.

7.   Robert Laughlin, *A Different Universe* (New York, NY: Basic
      Books, 2006).

8.   Robert J. Gordon, *The Rise and Fall of American Growth: The
      U.S. Standard of Living since the Civil War* (Princeton, NJ:
      Princeton University Press, 2016).

9.   Walter Bagehot, *Lombard Street: A Description of the Money
      Market* (London: Henry S. King, 1873), text available at the
      Library of Economics and Liberty, chapter I, paragraph 4 (http://
      www.econlib.org/library/Bagehot/bagLom1.html#).

CHAPTER 13: A WRINKLE IN TIME

1.   Alan Turing, *Systems of Logic Based on Ordinals*, quoted in
      George Dyson, *Turing's Cathedral* (New York, NY: Pantheon
      Books, 2012), 252. See also Gregory J. Chaitin, *Thinking about
      Gödel and Turing: Essays on Complexity, 1970–2007*
      (Hackensack, NJ: World Scientific Publishing, 2007).

2.   Ludwig von Mises as quoted in Israel M. Kirzner, *Ludwig von
      Mises* (Wilmington, DE: ISI Books, 2001), 72.

3.   "Life's Irreducible Structure," chapter 14 in Michael Polanyi,
      Knowing and Being: Essays by Michael Polanyi (Chicago, IL:
      University of Chicago Press, 1969), 225–39.

4. Thomas Piketty, *Capital in the Twenty-First Century* (Cambridge, MA: Harvard University Press, 2014), 264 and *passim*.

5. Adolf Hitler, *Mein Kampf*, chapter 12, as examined in "The Economics of Hate," chapter 5 in George Gilder, *The Israel Test: Why the World's Most Besieged State Is a Beacon of Freedom and Hope for the World Economy* (New York, NY: Encounter Books, 2012), 63–71.

6. Sadi Carnot et al., *Reflections on the Motive Power of Fire* (New York, NY: John Wiley & Sons, 1897 edition), http://books.google.com/books?id=tgdJAAAAIAAJ.

7. Nicholas Georgescu-Roegen, *The Entropy Law and the Economic Process* (Cambridge, MA: Harvard University Press, 1971). The new Malthusians make the argument that the ecological costs of capitalism, measurable through the entropy law, nullify net profits and thus render the system "unsustainable."

8. Cesar Hidalgo's mostly definitive *Why Information Grows: The Evolution of Order, from Atoms to Economies* (New York, NY: Basic Books, 2015) presents Ludwig Boltzmann as an advocate of information as order. But information theory treats information as disorder—unexpected rather than predictable results, measured by entropy, which in the theories of both Boltzmann and Shannon is the opposite of order.

9. Hubert P. Yockey, *Information Theory, Evolution, and the Origin of Life* (Cambridge: Cambridge University Press, 2005), 166.

10. "The Knowledge Horizon," chapter 24 in Gilder, *Knowledge and Power: The Information Theory of Capitalism and How It Is Revolutionizing Our World* (Washington, DC: Regnery Publishing, 2013), 257–72.

11. Dennis W. Sciama, *The Unity of the Universe* (Garden City, NY: Doubleday Anchor Books, 1959).

12. Robert P. Crease, *World in the Balance: The Historic Quest for an Absolute System of Measurement* (New York, NY: W. W. Norton, 2011), 261–64.

13. Richard Vigilante, personal communication.

CHAPTER 14: RESTORING REAL MONEY

1. Friedrich Hayek, "Toward a Free Market Monetary System," in James A. Dorn and Anna J. Schwartz, eds., *The Search for Stable Money* (Chicago, IL: University of Chicago Press, 1987), 383.

2. Arnold Kling, "Turning Guns to Butter: How Postwar America Brought the Boys Home without Bringing the Economy Down," *Reason*, October 12, 2010. Kling's larger theory is expounded in his definitive *Unchecked and Unbalanced: How the Discrepancy between Knowledge and Power Caused the Financial Crisis and Threatens Democracy* (Lanham, MD: Rowman & Littlefield, 2010). See also Robert Higgs, "Regime Uncertainty: Why the Great Depression Lasted So Long and Why Prosperity Resumed after the War," *Independent Review*, no. 4 (1997): 561–90.

3. Ed Conway, *The Summit: Bretton Woods 1944: J. M. Keynes and the Reshaping of the Global Economy* (New York, NY: Pegasus Books, 2015), epilogue.

4. Maurice McTigue, "Rolling Back Government, Lessons from New Zealand," Hillsdale College *Imprimis* 33, no. 4 (April 2004), .

5. George Gilder, *The Israel Test: Why the World's Most Besieged State Is a Beacon of Freedom and Hope for the World Economy* (New York, NY: Encounter Books, 2012).

6. Steve Forbes with Elizabeth Ames, *Reviving America: How Repealing Obamacare, Replacing the Tax Code, and Reforming the Fed will Restore Hope and Prosperity* (New York, NY: McGraw Hill Education, 2016), 124 and passim.

7.   Metcalfe's Law ordains that the power and value of a network rises roughly by the square of the number of compatible devices linked to it.

8.   Judy Shelton, *Fixing the Dollar Now: Why U.S. Money Lost Its Integrity and How We Can Restore It* (Washington, DC: Atlas Economic Research Foundation, 2011).

9.   Ibid., 40–44.

10. Ibid., 48, citing Alan Greenspan, "Can the U.S. Return to a Gold Standard?," *Wall Street Journal*, September 1, 1981.

Index